Coach Yourself to
SUCCESS

Coach Yourself to
SUCCESS

Winning the
Investment Game

Joe Moglia
CEO of Ameritrade Holding Corporation

WILEY

John Wiley & Sons, Inc.

Published by John Wiley & Sons, Inc., Hoboken, New Jersey.
Published simultaneously in Canada.

Library of Congress Cataloging-in-Publications Data

Moglia, Joe.
    Coach yourself to success / Joe Moglia.
      p. cm.
    Includes bibliographical references and index.
    ISBN-13 978-0-471-71984-7 (cloth)
    ISBN-10 0-471-71984-6 (cloth)
    1. Investments.   2. Stocks.   3. Bonds.   4. Mutual funds.   5. Cash management.
6. Finance, Personal. I. Title.
    HG4521.M64 2005
    332.6—dc22

                             2004028736

Printed in the United States of America
10 9 8 7 6 5 4 3 2 1

Dedicated
to my mother,

Frances McLarnon Moglia.

My inspiration,
my best friend,
and a beacon of light and hope.

CONTENTS

ABOUT THE AUTHOR

Joe Moglia is not your average Joe. He is the Chief Executive Officer of Ameritrade Holding Corporation. Ameritrade Inc., a subsidiary brokerage, is one of the largest online brokerage firms in the world. Since Joe took over the helm in 2001, the Omaha, Nebraska–based company has more than doubled its revenue and boosted net income by 1,000 percent. He currently serves on the boards of five community, academic, and financial institutions.

Prior to arriving at Ameritrade, Joe had a 17-year tenure at Merrill Lynch. Just four years after he joined Merrill in 1984, he was its top institutional salesperson. He ultimately worked his way through executive management positions on both the Institutional and Private Client sides of the firm. Before leaving, he was responsible for all private client investment products, the insurance company, the 401(k) business, and the middle-market business.

Before Joe entered the investment world, he was Football Defensive Coordinator at Dartmouth College. The team won two Ivy League championships in his three-year tenure there, capping his 16-year career as an educator and football coach. He authored, *The Key to Winning Football: The Perimeter Attack Offense*, as well as numerous articles in national coaching journals.

Despite all his accolades and achievements, Joe was far from being born with a platinum spoon in his mouth. He was born of immigrant parents, neither one of whom had the opportunity to go to high school. Seven family members grew up in a two-bedroom, one-bath apartment in the Dyckman Street section of Manhattan. His mother was a homemaker until the kids were grown, and his father owned a neighborhood fruit and grocery store. During high school, Joe played football and baseball, and also worked at his father's store. Already a married father by the age of 19, he took a job as an assistant football coach at his high school alma mater while attending Fordham University, continuing to put in hours at the family store. He received a bachelor's degree in economics from Fordham and a master's in secondary education from the University of Delaware.

Joe's passion was football and, after completing his education, he pursued a successful coaching career. Years later, seeing the toll that the travel and 90-hour work weeks were taking on his family, which by then included four young children, Joe decided to try his hand at another of his passions: business.

He entered Merrill Lynch's sales training class when he was 34 years old. There were 25 MBAs from the likes of Harvard and Stanford—and one football coach. He quickly moved into executive management.

Today, the father of four grown children and two teenage stepchildren, he lives in Omaha with his wife, Amy, a graphic artist. An exceptional businessman, coach, and mentor, Joe can truly understand the issues that plague most Americans. He grew up seeing what it is to struggle financially, and to worry about not having enough money to get by, let alone to save and invest. He knows that the sweetest success comes from grit, heart, and love—"putting others' needs before your own," as Joe defines it—whether "others" mean the family, the team, or the company.

Ever the educator and coach, Joe felt the need to divulge what other Wall Street wonders would just as soon keep under wraps—that investing can be manageable and you can master it on your own. He wanted to write this book for average people who find it overly complex to handle their own investments, so they either pay others a lot of money to do it for them or, worse yet, don't even have a portfolio in place. Joe believes that these people—people like *you*—are more than capable of creating and executing an investment plan, only they don't know it. It's called The Dorothy Principle. The girl born not too far from Omaha felt she needed a wizard to find her way home, but later she learned she had always possessed everything she needed to reach her destination: grit, heart, and love.

Joe knows you have what it takes, but just need a little guidance and coaching to gain a firm grasp of the investing basics that will help you reach *your* financial destination. He offers you the fundamentals, so you can utilize them to develop your investment game plan—not just for today's game, not just for next week's, but for next season's and for all the seasons of your life.

FOREWORD

Wall Street is jam-packed with financial products. In fact, it's as crowded out there as a public golf course on a weekend. So how can the average investor possibly be expected to filter through and select from among the thousands of investment options? Help is on the way. I'll tell you what questions you should be asking yourself and how the answers will help you zero in on the picks that are just right for you—and in just the right doses. Once the field of options has thinned, your course will be clear.

But before you can begin to really take charge of your financial future, let's first back up a bit. After all, hopefully, you wouldn't even be playing any sport in the first place if you didn't have the right equipment and knew, at the very least, the basics of the game. It's the same with investing. There are millions of people divvying up their holdings while lacking a basic knowledge of the fundamentals. Without a firm grasp on the different asset classes and how well suited they are to meet your goals, the price you pay may be steep. At best, your money may not grow as fast as it could; at worst, you could end up losing much of your hard-earned nest egg. Once you've read this book, not only will you have a better idea of what to do, you'll have a better understanding of why you're doing it.

It's essential to first have a thorough understanding of the different tools available to build a well-balanced portfolio. Most everyone has heard of stocks, bonds, and mutual funds, and many have at least heard of exchange-traded funds. But do you know how these products differ in terms of risk, cost, and tax consequences—as well as other characteristics? Once I've explained the subtle—and even the not so subtle—distinctions, I'll show you how to put those tools to work for you in the most cost-efficient, productive way. You'll select investments factoring in your individual timeline and a level of risk that will allow you to sleep well at night. And you'll know how to finish this sentence: The *single* most important action you should take to bolster long-term returns is _____. (Hint: it *isn't* picking this year's hottest mutual fund.) Find the answer in Chapter 8. With the information in this book under your belt, you'll have all the knowledge you need to construct and execute your personal investment plan.

Why am I taking the time and trouble to write this book? Because I care. Yes, I know it sounds corny, but it's the truth. I'm very committed to the client experience and want you to have a solid understanding of the core investment principles so you can make informed, intelligent decisions about your and your family's financial future.

I agree wholeheartedly and feel so strongly about helping the investor achieve his goals that I want you to succeed—no matter where you decide to park and grow your money.

So read the book. Understand your choices. Understand yourself as an investor. Understand which selections are right for you and how to apportion your nest egg among a multitude of just the right type and number of baskets. Then set your selections on automatic and let them ride, checking back now and then to make sure you haven't veered off course. Got a question? I'll tell you where to turn for help, but I'm confident the groundwork of investing basics that follows will act as a compass, helping you to navigate the sometimes-turbulent investment waters and keeping you on track until you achieve your goals.

Joe Moglia
CEO of Ameritrade

Note: We will be covering many different kinds of investment products, all with unique characteristics and risks. A couple of specific disclosures are warranted.

For *investment companies*, like mutual funds and exchange-traded funds that have a prospectus or product description, it is important to know that:

- *Before investing in any investment company, be sure to carefully consider the particular company's investment objectives, risks, charges, and expenses involved. A prospectus contains this and other important information, and should be read carefully before investing. You can obtain a prospectus from the investment company directly, or from your broker.*
- International investments involve special risks, including currency fluctuations, and political and economic instability.
- And let's not forget one of the most important rules in financial circles, as in sports, past performance does not guarantee future results.

ACKNOWLEDGMENTS

A s with any great team, it is the group of individuals that make the team successful. I would like to thank Joe Ricketts for encouraging me to get in the game and write this book; also, I would like to thank Mike Feigeles and Scott Parry who got us to mid-field, Anne Nelson and Doug Smith who got us to the ten and Donna Kush, Tim Smith, Phyllis Nelson, and Bill Sampson who took us into the end zone. Ellen Koplow kept us on plan and moving forward.

Finally, my personal and special thanks to Marcy Tolkoff who helped create the ingenious game plan that allowed us to win.

Coach Yourself to
SUCCESS

PART ONE

The Basic Tools of Investing

THE PREGAME SHOW

You're about to enter the world of investing. It's a lot like sports and a lot like life. Some of it is as dull as watching paint dry, while other aspects are thrilling and can truly make your heart race with excitement.

This book is divided into two parts. At the risk of making my editor angry, I've got to be honest with you: The first part is, well, a bit boring. Basically, it describes the building blocks of investing and the primary types of assets, so you can understand what each one is and how it differs from the rest. Part Two is the fun part, where you put your understanding to work and see how the pieces of the puzzle come together to create a beautiful vista of the investment field.

I tried to make Part One as interesting as possible, but it's tough to jazz up the fundamentals. Imagine this: You sit down in front of the television, snacks at the ready, all pumped up to see a close football game between two great teams. You turn to the channel and see training camp, with the players doing push-ups, wind sprints, and sit-ups. Conditioning—without which any player would be useless—can be a real snooze to watch. So can physical therapy or rehab. Or picture a classroom, where everyone is viewing game films and staring at a blackboard with Xs and Os, having plays drilled into their heads.

I know there are some diehards out there like me that'll love that, but it's not exactly great entertainment.

Compare that to sitting down in front of the television, reveling in the excitement of watching two talented professional, college, or high school teams. The masterful running, powerful blocking, and soaring passes are like poetry in motion.

My point? You can't possibly have a Part Two without first having a Part One, any more than you can have a great football match-up without seasoned players who are in shape and well versed in the fundamental aspects of the game. So bear with Part One—skim it if you absolutely must—but I'm telling you that the more closely you read it, the more you'll understand and appreciate not only Part Two, but the arena of investing as a whole.

Ready? It's game-time!

"Coach" Joe Moglia,
CEO of Ameritrade

chapter one
STOCKS

Why We Own Them

Stock *n* 1: the proprietorship element in a corporation usually divided
into shares and represented by transferable certificates.
            Source: Merriam-Webster's Collegiate Dictionary, 11th edition

A share of stock represents equity, or ownership, in a company. Even
if you own a single share, you're still a part owner. A small part, true,
but an owner nonetheless. If you've never really understood the
nature of stock and how it comes into existence, you're in good company. Millions of intelligent adults never got "the talk" from their
parents about the financial facts of life. If you're one of them, here's
how stock is "born."

Let's say 21-year-old twin brothers Willy and Wally Widget
invent an ingenious item. They name the invention after themselves
and, with some seed money from their Uncle William, start manufacturing widgets on a small scale. The venture is a huge success and
sales go through the roof, as the media can speak of nothing but the
Widget wunderkinder. Eager to raise money to build new factories
and take the company to a whole new level, the savvy Widget boys
decide to offer part of their company to the public—for a price.

A large investment bank or brokerage firm underwrites the initial public offering (IPO) of shares to a few select clients—mostly large institutional investors—at a given price and the Widgets get the much-needed capital to expand and grow their business. After the shares are sold to the initial investors, they're traded on the open, or secondary, market, where anyone can buy them. The value of a share is no longer fixed, but goes up and down, depending upon the company's financial health and those other famous twins, Supply and Demand. And that's how stock makes its way into the financial world.

Over 84 million individuals in the United States own stock, or equities, either directly or through stock mutual funds (we'll get to those later on).[1] What's the big attraction? Well, there's always the fantasy that you'll be the one to scoop up one million shares of say, Widget, at $5.00 a share, before the general public catches on and it soars to $120 a share. Of course, we've all heard stories of this kind of luck and it sometimes happens. So do lottery jackpots. However, you can't bank on them. But if you do some digging and make prudent choices, you should reasonably be able to count on the earnings from:

Growth stocks. Companies that still have a lot of growing to do typically put profits back into the business and are referred to as "growth" stocks. These have generally outperformed their peers in past earnings and are expected to continue to do so in the future.

When the share price goes up, your capital has appreciated: that is, your investment has increased in value. Of course, you don't really capture, or realize, that gain, until you sell the stock. It's the same in the unfortunate case the stock price goes down—the loss is merely on paper until the shares are sold.

Income stocks. An investor can bolster his/her income through a payout of company profits, or dividends. Typically, large established businesses like utilities and some banks are the most likely to distribute profits. The average shareholder holds what's called "common" stock, in which he or she may receive quarterly dividend distributions, as well as the right to have a vote on important company matters— like electing a board of directors. The greater the distribution, the greater the income.

Institutional and very affluent individual shareholders are more likely to own "preferred" stock. These stockholders are in line before common stockholders when it comes to getting some money back should the company go belly up, plus they get first dibs on dividends. However, preferred shareholders only receive a set amount; they won't reap added rewards should there be a boost in profits.

If you're nearing retirement and are concerned about increasing your income flow, or if you're just a conservative investor who would secretly prefer to keep his or her money in the cookie jar, consider a *dividend reinvestment plan* (DRIP or DRP). In these programs, you regularly buy shares of stock—minimizing or waiving trading costs—in the sturdy heavyweights that have solid histories of distributing dividends.

Have the dividends reinvested to buy more shares of stock if you don't need the income right away. This is a savvy way to buy more stock and it's called *dollar-cost averaging*. Since share prices go up and down, your continued flow of dollars back into the company will buy you more shares when the price is down and fewer shares when the price goes up. The average price per share that you'll pay will be lower with dollar-cost averaging; it's a safeguard against our natural human impulse to buy more stock when it's going up and less when the price is down. (If the stock continues to go down, do additional research.) Another way to reap high dividends is to buy what are called the *Dogs of the Dow*, the 10 highest-yielding stocks on the Dow Jones Industrial Average (more on this later).

Value stocks are those whose worth is not fully reflected in their share price. A company may be undervalued if it has gone through hard times and experts believe it will turn around. Perhaps the employees were on strike or there was a public relations disaster, such as the case of Johnson & Johnson (JNJ) and the Tylenol tampering in 1982. For a while, JNJ was practically a dirty word in the pharmaceutical industry. But it was a strong company with solid fundamentals at its core. Smart *value investors* bought the stock after the price plunged, believing that the company would right itself and regain its former stature—which is precisely what happened.

Spotting a Stock that Is Ripe for the Picking

How can you tell which stocks are going to be moneymakers? This is the $64,000 question—and, sometimes, it's worth much more than that. Start by logging onto the top financial Web sites (see Resources at the end of this book). You'll see experts' recommendations for stocks that have a great deal of future potential. But it's wise to do some research on your own. The average person will probably find it difficult to grasp the accounting principles necessary to truly understand a company's balance sheets. The good news? It doesn't matter one bit. You don't need to be a certified public accountant or financial planner to spot a promising investment—and you don't have to pay through the nose to have someone do it for you.

A good way to begin evaluating whether a stock is a smart prospect is to research it at financial Web sites such as Morningstar.com. (ValueLine.com is another research starting point.) You'll need to enter the company's ticker symbol, which is a combination of one or a few letters that signifies the company's name. Usually, it's an abbreviation of sorts, but not always. Let's say you enter WDG (for Widget) in the search bar.

The first piece of information you want to find is its P/E, or price to earnings ratio. That means:

$$\text{P/E Ratio} = \frac{\text{Price per share}}{\text{Annual earnings per share}}$$

The lower the company's earnings relative to the price of the stock, the higher the P/E. A high P/E may mean the stock is either overvalued or overpriced. If the earnings per share are 10 cents and the share price is $15.00, that means a whopping P/E of 150! Your goal is to find a stock that has yet to reach its potential.

You'll get a better sense of where a company typically stands if you look at the historical, or past years', P/E and compare that to the current figure. Don't be guided solely by the most recent earnings, since one or two quarters may have been exceptionally good—or bad—and may not reflect general performance. When it comes to growth stocks, you also want to look at the rate at which profits grow, or the earnings growth rate; ideally, the P/E ratio should be lower than the growth rate, which means the stock is undervalued. An attractive P/E ratio should be comparable to or less than the P/E of the industry (in Widget's case, that is manufacturing).

Another indicator of financial health is the *price-book ratio*; instead of comparing the share price to earnings, this compares the price to the company's assets, also called its *book value*. Investors looking for a bargain seek out stocks selling for less than their book value. So do corporate raiders who look for companies that might be ripe for an acquisition, after which parts of the company can be sold off for a profit.

Financial websites generally will give you a stocks five-year P/E ratio, as well as suggested price points at which to buy, and sell, and an estimate of the stock's fair market value. Morningstar for example uses a star rating (five stars is the highest) and letter grading that evaluates stocks according to their growth, valuation and, financial health.

Let's say there isn't such an obvious reason for a company being undervalued or even for determining that's the case in the first place. How would you know? Rather than go through a complicated analysis to determine the value of a company's worth relative to its price, look to Morningstar's analysis of 1,000 stocks. It identifies them as value or growth, and specifies the size according to *market cap*. A company's market capitalization is the number of shares outstanding multiplied by the share price. *Large-cap* stocks are companies with capitalizations of over $5 billion; *mid-caps*, between $1.5 and 5 billion; and *small-caps*, less than $1.5 billion.

Investing rule #1: You *never* want to own just one type of stock (or just one type of any asset class, for that matter). The stock market goes in cycles. When large companies are thriving, small and medium-sized ones tend to experience down times. Size really does matter when it comes to constructing a portfolio of stocks. You want to have a mix not only of size, but also of growth and value, because when one group is underperforming, it's likely that the other group is doing well.

You should also make sure your holdings reflect a mix of the different sectors, or segments, of the economy, since they, too, go in cycles. If you own a stock in a high-performing sector, you'll do very well; if you own a stock in a poor-performing sector, you won't do well. Own stock in both sectors and you'll likely do well over time. Morningstar recognizes 12 sectors: Software, Hardware, Media, Telecom, Healthcare, Consumer Services, Business Services, Financial Services, Consumer Goods, Industrial Materials, Energy, and Utilities. Specific industries are mapped to one of the 12 sectors. For example, Citigroup is in the "International Banks" industry within the "Financial Services" sector.

An important way of evaluating a stock's performance is to compare it to the market as a whole, or more narrowly, the segment that reflects similarly sized companies. Generally, investors compare a stock's performance and P/E to that of an index. Indexes give an overall sense of how the stock market—or portions of it—is performing.

The first stock index was created by Charles Dow and Edward Jones. They picked 12 large industrial companies and, in 1896, began publishing the daily status of their stock prices. By tracking the performance of these businesses, investors could assess the state of the economy. The list grew to 30 "blue chip" companies and became known as the Dow Jones Industrial Average (DJIA).

Trivia tidbit: the only company of the original 12 still in the DJIA is General Electric.[2]

The Standard & Poor's 500 Index (called the S&P for short), tracks a broad base of 500 widely held companies and is the primary benchmark used by most investors. It's calculated so the companies considered bellwethers of the marketplace have more weight than other companies. The NASDAQ 100 tracks those, mostly tech, stocks that trade through its electronic system. Then there's the Russell 2000 which tracks primarily small- and mid-sized companies, and the Wilshire 5000, considered to be the broadest index of all since it tracks the stock of the vast majority of public companies. Of course, there are many other indexes; these are just the major ones.

Aside from comparison to an index, there are also other subjective criteria for deciding whether to invest in a stock. Investment guru Warren Buffett won't invest in a company if he doesn't understand the nature of the business. His company's holdings include such known commodities as Coca-Cola, Gillette and American Express.[3] Not a "techie," he was ridiculed for refusing to go along in the tech-wild late 1990s. But when millions of investors lost their shirts at the end of the decade, guess who had the last laugh. If you're an automobile salesman, and are sensing a shift in the industry toward say, electric cars, you might want to invest in a company that's at the forefront of the trend. Go with what you know and know what you own.

Randi G. had a hunch that change would soon be in the air after Florida's presidential election debacle in November of 2000. When she read about a company that makes new and improved voting machines, she decided to invest, feeling certain there would be a strong need for

new machines by states seeking to modernize their voting equipment.
As it turns out, she was right. After the share price went up 30 percent,
she sold out and kept a tidy little profit.

Where Stocks Are Bought and Sold

Before you can begin to invest, you have to open a brokerage
account. There are a few different options available to you. We'll get
into this in much greater detail in Chapter 10, but, in a nutshell, the
least expensive route is an online brokerage firm. Here you can buy
and sell for less than $11 a pop and have access to third-party invest-
ment research. Full-service brokerage firms will charge you a flat fee,
a commission of about $100 per trade, or both. In return, you should
expect to receive lots of investment guidance and direction as far as
which stocks are better buys than others.

The majority of stocks are sold on one of three *exchanges*. Think
of an exchange like a shopping mall, except there are no chain stores.
If you want to buy from the Widget store, for example, you can do so
only at the exchange where that company, or "store," is located.

The most well-known exchange is the New York Stock Exchange (NYSE), or "Big Board." About 5,767 large companies trade
on the NYSE where trades are executed auction-style.[4] A specialist on the floor of the exchange must match up a buyer whose *bid*
meets the seller's *ask price*. The American Stock Exchange (AMEX)
primarily lists small- and medium-sized companies. Then there's
the National Association of Security Dealers Automated Quotations (NASDAQ), where much but not all of the listed companies
involve technology. NASDAQ doesn't have a trading floor; instead,
it links buyers and sellers via computer where trades are placed
electronically.

How to Place a Trade

Market orders are the most common. This means that the broker should buy or sell at whatever the share price is when the order is actually executed. So if the price is listed at $15.25 when you decide to buy, and in the span of time between when you placed the order and when it's filled the price has risen to $15.30, the price you pay is $15.30.

Limit orders are placed when you don't want to buy or sell unless the share is at a set price. If you want to buy a stock for $46 a share but it now sells for $50, you can place a limit order at $46. If the stock falls below $46, the broker will buy shares for you at the lower price, and you'll save the difference. It works the same on the up side. Say you wanted to sell a stock if it reaches $50 but is now selling for $46. The stock shoots up to $53, the broker sells your shares, and you make even more than you'd originally hoped. All price limit orders carry the risk of missing the market altogether.

Stop orders are placed when the stock hits a target price, to protect a profit or stem a loss. If you bought a stock at $50 and it's gone up to $75, you could place a stop-loss order at $65. That means your broker will sell your shares at whatever the price is once it dips below $65. If a tornado flattens the company's main factory and shares plunge to $60, you'll have preserved $10 of your per share profit before the shares drop further.

Trading Strategies

For the vast majority of investors, stocks should be bought for the long term—not for an hour or a day. Not that there's anything inherently wrong with active or day-trading. It's just that it requires a great deal of savvy—and luck. Investors are forever trying to time the market, that is, to anticipate precisely which stocks will go up—and when. And, although it's possible to be successful every once in awhile, it's extraordinarily difficult to do on a consistent basis. History shows that if you jumped in and out of the market in an attempt to anticipate market upticks, over time, you would have lost a great deal of money, compared to a buy-and-hold investor. So unless you're a pro or have decided to take a small portion, say five percent, of your assets to "play" with, you don't want to act on a supposedly hot tip from Day-trade Dave in your office or something you read on the *ItIsYourLuckyDay.com* Web site.

However, if you get weak in the knees simply thinking about a drop in the stock market, skip to the next section. *Buying on margin* and *selling short* are speculative trading strategies, and neither is intended for the faint of heart. With both, you borrow money from a broker. When you buy on margin, you should have a very good reason to believe a stock price is going to rise but don't want to put up all the money to buy shares. Using other securities as collateral, a broker loans you the money, allowing you to buy the number of shares you want. Hopefully, the stock shoots up quickly, you sell the shares, pay off the margin loan—with interest—and walk off with a nice profit.

As you know, however, stocks don't always behave the way we would like. If the price of the shares falls or doesn't rise as high as expected, you won't earn enough to repay the loan and interest. Worst-case scenario: If the stock falls by half, you'll be faced with the dreaded margin call, which strikes terror in the heart of even the most stalwart market player. A margin call means you'll need to come up with more collateral to cover the greater potential loss and you could lose your entire investment as well and have other securities sold to cover the debt.

Selling short is a different sort of a tactic. Unlike the usual scenario—where you buy a stock hoping the price will go up—you short a stock because you believe the price will go *down*. Here's how it works: You borrow shares from a broker and sell them. When the price drops, you buy them back at the lower price, pocketing the difference, minus interest and the broker's commission. Again, if the stock misbehaves and actually increases in value, you lose. And since there is no limit to how high the stock price could climb, your loss is potentially unlimited. Considering that, over time, stocks generally trend upward, it's a whole lot wiser to preserve—not imperil—your nest egg.

Finally, let's just make note of trading strategies from a *tax* perspective. Short-term gains—those on sales of stock held less than one year—are taxed at your higher ordinary income tax rate. If you had owned the stock for over a year, you would pay the more favorable capital gains tax rate. So if you've decided to sell a stock and have owned it for almost a year, consider holding on a bit longer until you're past the 365-day mark; consult your tax advisor for individual advice.

Also, be aware of the "wash-sale" rule: Let's say you want to take a loss to offset your gains, which would reduce your ordinary income and, therefore, the amount of taxes you'll owe. The concept is a good one and practiced by savvy stock traders everywhere. However, in this example, you sell the stock to take the loss, but you believe the stock will rally and want to buy it right back again at the now-low price (as opposed to the higher purchase price when you bought it the first time). If you buy it back within 30 days of the sale, the IRS won't let you take the loss, since they see it more as profiteering than really having a loss. Of course, you could take the loss if you wait 31 days...

When to Hold, When to Fold

Let's assume you researched the company and believed in its future potential before you decided to invest. Experts suggest that when you buy a sound investment, you should hold for a long time. How long is long? Well, billionaire investor Warren Buffett's notorious reply to that question is "forever." I don't think the answer is quite so black and white, though. Ask yourself:

- Has there been an acquisition, merger, or other change in management?
- Has there been a major development in the industry that would alter the company's prospects?
- Are lots of company insiders selling their shares? This is not necessarily a sign you should sell. It could be that insiders need to free up cash for personal reasons, completely unrelated to company performance. It's just one factor to look at among many others.
- Has the company drastically cut or stopped paying dividends? This may be a sign of trouble. It may also be a sign that profits are being redirected for perfectly legitimate, financially sound reasons. Read what management has to say about it in the company's public filings and annual report.
- Did you already reach your target price? Many investors have a certain gain in mind—say, 30 percent—above the purchase price. If so, this is a legitimate reason to take your profit off the table.
- Has this stock grown so that it now represents a greater portion of your portfolio than it should? This relates to asset allocation and rebalancing, which we'll talk more about in Chapters 8 and 9.
- How is the company performing compared to the rest of the sector? If its industry cousins are thriving, that might signal a

problem. *What about the market as a whole?* If the entire market is stormy, that isn't a good reason to jump ship. Jonathan Pond, investment advisor and author of *Your Money Matters*, notes, "As the saying goes, you don't complain about your stateroom on the Titanic."[5] So if all stocks are sinking, don't pull out of one company and risk missing out on potential gains down the road when the market turns around.

Answering the above questions and evaluating the company's present status can help you determine if your money would be put to better use in another company's stock—or in another asset class altogether. This brings us to the next chapter.

Coach Moglia's Game Plan

1. *Invest for the long-term.* Don't listen to hot stock tips. Don't try to time the market by jumping into and out of stocks after a few days or weeks. And don't sell stocks short, hoping they'll go down. Leave all that to professional traders.

2. *Buy a mix of stocks.* Balance your portfolio with stocks from different sectors of the economy. And buy different-sized companies—choosing from the so-called large-, mid-, and small-cap groups. That way, you won't get burned when a certain sector drops in value.

3. *Unless you have a good reason, don't sell for at least a year.* If you hold a stock for 365 days before selling, you'll likely pay *substantially* less tax on your gains.

chapter two
BONDS

Bonds are the Rodney Dangerfield of investments. They just don't get much respect. Stocks are the prettier sister and garner most of the attention, while bonds are viewed as ultra-conservative and, let's face it, plain ol' boring. But not everyone is put off by bonds' image problem. In fact, the *truly* moneywise know that bond ownership can be quite lucrative.

> Bond *n* 1: an interest-bearing certificate of public or private indebtedness 2: an insurance agreement pledging surety for financial loss caused to another by the act of default or a third person or by some contingency over which the third person may have no control.
> *Source:* Merriam-Webster's Collegiate Dictionary, 11th edition

There aren't many guarantees in this world. In fact, you've heard the old saying that the only two things you can count on are death and taxes. Well, there's a third that comes pretty close: certain types of *fixed-income securities*, especially government-backed bonds. *Fixed* income: It even *sounds* secure.

Investment experts agree that fixed-income securities should be a component of almost every investor's portfolio. First, they temper the volatility of equities, since the two asset classes generally tend to move in opposite directions. When stocks were sky-high in the late 1990s, no one was talking much about bonds. But in the two years following March of 2000 when the tech bubble burst, bonds were all the rage.

They're also an excellent income-booster for those who hold them until maturity and for investors nearing retirement. Finally, bonds can provide capital appreciation for investors who trade them at a profit.

Basic Bond Features

Generally referred to as bonds, fixed-income investments are essentially IOUs. Think of the mortgage on your house, except in the case of bonds, *you're* the bank! Here's how it works: You agree to lend money (*principal*) for a set time period (*term*) to the government or a corporation seeking to raise capital to either finance future growth or pay off existing debts. You buy the bond typically in units of $1,000 at par (*face value*), below par (*discount*) or above par (*premium*).

The debtor agrees to pay you interest (*coupon*) at a specified rate and intervals.

> *Trivia tidbit: Interest is referred to as the coupon because, in the old days, a bond came with actual coupons attached; in order to receive your interest payment, you had to submit a coupon.*[1]

A $20,000, 10-year bond with a coupon rate of 5 percent will pay $1,000 a year, or 5 percent of $20,000. When the loan term ends (*maturity date*), you receive the face value, as well as any interest still owed.

One type of security is sold below par and doesn't provide for any interest payments at all until the maturity date, when all the interest is paid in a lump sum—an amount that, when added to the discounted purchase price, equals the bond's face value. It's called a *zero-coupon* bond for a very logical reason: Until the maturity date, you get zero. There are also bonds that provide for a combination of periodic interest payments with partial lump-sum payments at the end of the term.

Aside from payment terms, another important feature is the *call* option, which means the issuer has the right to buy back a bond issue before its maturity date. A predetermined call option may be built in or triggered by the occurrence of certain events. If your bond's issue has a call option, you'll want to know if it provides for a *sinking fund,* where assets are set aside to ensure that investors will be repaid.

All the particulars of a bond are laid out at the onset and generally don't change, hence the term "fixed" income. You can purchase newly issued "on the run" securities via auction through the government's TreasuryDirect program (*www.publicdebt.treas.gov*). Those already in the secondary market are bought or sold through a bond trader or brokerage firm.

Bonds in the Marketplace

Bonds are traded over-the-counter, not on an exchange, but the concept is similar to stocks in terms of matching up an *ask price* with a *bid price*. Any difference between the ask and bid price is called the *spread*. Interest rates and bond price have an inverse relationship: When rates go down, the price goes up. Let's say you bought a bond when interest rates were 10 percent and rates later plummet to 5 percent. Since the coupon rate on the bond you own remains at 10 percent, investors are willing to pay more than the face value for the bond. Demand goes up and so does the price.

Unlike stocks, you can't look to a ticker tape to get a precise read on the market value of your bonds. This lack of "price transparency" plagued investors for years. In an effort to get a handle on bond prices, the Bond Market Association created its Web site, *www. investinginbonds.com*, where certain bond prices are provided—primarily those of bonds in large supply that trade frequently. You can also track historical performance of specific issues as well as similar issues to see how yours stack up.

At the crux of determining a bond's fluctuating value is its yield, or rate of return. The current yield is the annual interest divided by the bond's price. The higher the bond's purchase price is over par, the lower the current yield and vice versa. Another way to assess a bond's value and a benchmark used for trading is its Yield to Maturity (YTM). This is a complicated formula that assumes reinvestment of all interest at the same rate and ownership until maturity.

Whether you're a trader or an investor holding a bond until maturity, it's important to understand the yield curve, a chart that plots the relationship between bond yields and maturity lengths. It can give you insight into market trends and help guide you as to whether and when to buy or sell your securities. In order to induce investors to lock up their money for the long haul, interest rates on long-term securities are generally higher than those on short-term securities. Therefore, a *normal yield curve* slopes upward, where bonds with the shortest maturities have the lowest yield and those with the longest maturities have the highest (see Figure 2.1a). A *flat yield curve* makes no such distinction. You may find that, once the curve flattens, it no longer makes sense to hold fast to long-term bonds (see Figure 2.1b). An *inverted yield curve* reflects a Bizarro world, where everything is operating in reverse: Short-term bonds have the higher yields and long-term the lowest. This situation is an anomaly, usually doesn't last long, and making decisions at that time can be hazardous to your wealth (see Figure 2.1c).

You can sidestep trading altogether and opt for the more conservative buy-and-hold strategy of creating a *bond ladder* to boost yields

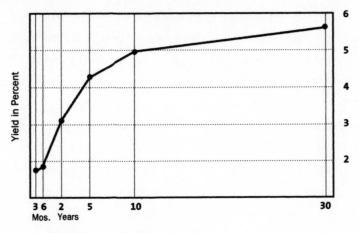

FIGURE 2.1a   Bonds: Normal Yield Curve
Source: Bloomberg

without taking on much risk. Let's say you have $100,000. Divide it up and buy ten $10,000 bonds, so that each one matures a year after the preceding one, that is: a one-year T-note, two-year, and so on. You get to take advantage of higher rates on longer-term notes. If rates go up even higher, you'll soon have a note coming due to take advantage

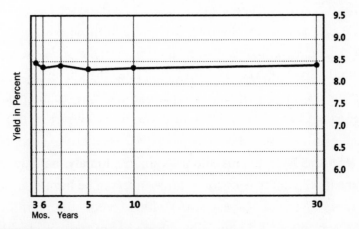

FIGURE 2.1b   Bonds: Flat Yield Curve
Source: Bloomberg

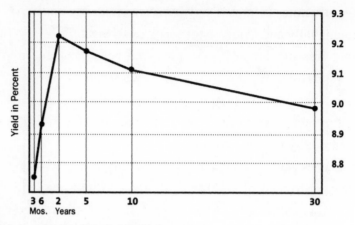

FIGURE 2.1c   Bonds: Inverted Yield Curve
Source: Bloomberg

of those higher rates. Should rates dip, only 1/10 of your money will be locked into a lower rate.

Bond Issuers

U.S. Treasury

Uncle Sam wants *you*—to loan him money! Primarily, he needs your help to pay off the national debt incurred as a result of borrowing money from other investors. Borrowing more money to pay off prior loans is called deficit financing. The three most common types of Treasuries are:

1. *Bonds* (30-year terms and a required $1,000 minimum investment).
2. *Notes* (2-, 5- or 10-year terms with a $5,000 minimum).
3. *Bills* (4-week, 3-month, 6-month, or 1-year terms, and a $10,000 minimum).

Treasury notes (T-notes) and Treasury bonds (T-bonds) pay interest semiannually and the investor receives the security's face value at maturity. Treasury bills (T-bills), are sold below par and don't pay any interest. However, at maturity, you receive the face value; the difference between the discount purchase price and the face value is the "interest." Income from all three is taxable by the federal government, but not by the city or state.

Treasuries held to maturity are basically a no-risk investment, since they're backed by the full faith and credit of the federal government. That means you're guaranteed repayment with the agreed-upon interest; even if Uncle Sam does not have the money to make good, he has the authority to raise taxes to generate the needed funds. Since Treasury bonds are so safe, their interest rates are lower than those of other bonds.

So if you're looking for a wild ride, look elsewhere, but keep in mind that some of the smartest money around is on these guaranteed debt instruments. Take Alan Greenspan, chairman of the Federal Reserve, for example. The man knows a thing or two about every type of investment, yet 96 percent of his reported wealth is invested in T-bills![2]

STRIPS are the U.S. Treasury's Separate Trade of Registered Interest and Principal of Securities. Whew! They're the government's "brand" of zero-coupon bonds. STRIPS are like T-bills in that the bond is bought at a deep discount, way below par. The coupon is "stripped" away although it continues to accrue. Then, at the maturity date, you receive all the interest, along with the original principal in one lump sum, which will equal the par value of the bond—your reward for foregoing years of interest payments.

TIPS (Treasury Inflation-Protected Securities) are the babies of the bond family, having only been introduced in 1997. These securities were created to thrive on inflation, which boosts the securities' principal and interest payments. The inflation rate is adjusted semi-annually and is pegged to the Consumer Price Index. It also has a built-in guarantee: even if there's *deflation*, you won't get back less than the TIPS' face value.

Savings Bonds

Savings bonds are securities that can only be issued by the Treasury and may not be traded, resold, or given to anyone other than the person named on them. *Series EE Savings Paper Bond*s are the most popular Treasury issue, partially because they can be purchased pretty cheaply. They're sold for half the face value, in denominations ranging from $50 up to $10,000. Interest is calculated as 90 percent of six-month five-year Treasury Securities yields. It accrues monthly and is compounded semiannually.

Savings bonds mature at varying dates, depending upon the date of issue, and they earn interest for 30 years. They can be redeemed once they've been held for 12 months, but if you hold them for fewer than five years from the issue date, you'll be hit with an early redemption penalty equal to three months' earned interest.

You receive your earnings as well as the bond's full face value upon maturity and must pay federal tax on those earnings upon redemption. An exception: They're exempt from federal tax if you use the earnings to pay for qualified higher education expenses and meet the income guidelines. All savings bond earnings are exempt from state and local income taxes.

They're easy to buy, with a purchase price as little as $25, either through an online account at TreasuryDirect, via automatic withdrawal with the Payroll Savings Plan, or at almost any bank.

The *Patriot Bond* is the Series EE Savings Bond with a patriotic emblem. It was introduced after 9/11, after many Americans expressed a desire to support the fight against terrorism. The reality is that the proceeds from all Treasury securities go into a general fund and are not specifically earmarked for antiterrorism efforts, although some of the money ends up being apportioned for that cause. Unlike traditional Series EE Savings Bonds, these cannot be purchased through Payroll Savings Plans, as they aren't set up to inscribe the Patriot emblem.

The *I-bond* was specifically created to help minimize the effects of inflation. It has two components: a fixed rate of return and a variable rate that represent a hedge against inflation, as measured by the Consumer Price Index.[3] I-bonds are sold at face value: A $500 bond costs $500.

Municipal Bonds

Whoever came up with the saying, "you can't judge a book by its cover" must have been thinking of municipal bonds (*munis*). These securities, issued by state and local governments, school districts, and other public entities, are usually bypassed by investors who do their bond shopping only by looking on the surface at the yield. Munis are generally exempt from federal taxes, as well as city or state tax if you're a resident of the city or state where the bond is issued. This is a crucial advantage that must be factored in when weighing one bond against another.

On the face of it, a five percent muni may look the same as a five percent taxable bond, right? But a five percent return sans city, state, and federal taxes, can turn into a *real* return of eight percent or more. In order to compare apples to apples, plug in the information at the Bond Marketing Association's Web site, *www.investinginbonds.com*, where there's a calculator to help you make the comparison.

Of course, there's an exception for every rule and munis are no different. If any of the interest is generated by what the tax law considers to be *private activity*—a charter school, for example—it may trigger the Alternative Minimum Tax (AMT), an alternate calculation less favorable to the taxpayer. Ask your bond dealer or brokerage firm to find out if the bond you're considering contains interest from private activity; this information is stated in the bond offering.

There is enormous variation among munis; you should consider their call options, interest payment intervals, and taxable status. Log onto *www.emuni.com* to learn more. Every investor should seriously consider whether to include them in the fixed-income portion of his or her taxable portfolio.

Government-Sponsored Enterprises

Government-sponsored enterprises (GSEs) are associations chartered or sponsored by the federal government. The best known are the housing associations: Federal National Mortgage Association (Fannie Mae), Federal Home Loan Mortgage Association (Freddie Mac), and General National Mortgage Association (Ginnie Mae). They buy large numbers of mortgages from banks, then pool them together and sell them as "mortgage-backed securities," which the consumer can then purchase from a bond dealer or a brokerage firm.

Their risk is slightly higher than Treasuries, since most GSEs are not backed by the full faith and credit of the federal government, but they're generally considered very safe securities. There is, however, some uncertainty as far as how much interest you'll earn. Owners of these securities receive monthly interest and principal of varying amounts (just like a mortgage payment). If mortgage interest rates fall and mortgagors refinance to lower their monthly payments, the owners of mortgage-backed securities will earn less interest.

Collaterized mortgage obligations (CMOs) are cousins to the traditional mortgage-backed securities. Issued by Freddie Mac, they pay interest and principal, but with greater certainty as to the size and timing of payments. In exchange for more predictability, yields are slightly lower. They're fairly complex instruments requiring a good degree of savvy and are better left to the experienced investor.

There are other GSEs as well, such as the Student Loan Marketing Association (Sallie Mae), which funds loan to college students, and the Farm Credit System (FCS), which loans money to farmers.

Corporations

It's common for corporations to use bonds as a way of raising money for expansion and growth. Of course, they can also issue more company stock to raise capital, but may prefer to borrow the money through bonds so it doesn't dilute the value of the stock shares already in the marketplace.

You have to be especially careful when buying corporate bonds. The most important criteria to look at when evaluating a corporation (or a muni) is its credit rating. A company called "high-yield" is also called "junk." That should tell you something. Consider a secured corporate bond, in which a company has backed up its bond with collateral, such as a mortgage or equipment. After all, if you shoot for high yields and the company defaults, your investment may very well be worthless. Another consideration: Unlike Treasuries and many munis, corporate bonds are generally subject to federal, state, and local tax.

Bond Ratings

While stocks are "rated" or evaluated by Morningstar, Value Line, and others, bonds are rated as well, so prospective investors can assess the level of risk before buying. The three main rating agencies are Moody's, Standard & Poor's, and Fitch Ratings. Corporate, municipal, and international bonds are rated, but not Treasuries. They automatically receive the highest rating (AAA), since they have the government's "money-back" guarantee (see Table 2.1).

The lower the rating, the higher the risk and the interest rate. If you opt for a higher interest rate by buying a bond with a "B" rating, that means there's a possibility that the debtor may default, in which case you'd lose your original principal. A rating of "CCC" means an even higher interest rate, but it also signifies that a company or municipality may be on the cusp of defaulting. Risk can be its own reward, but it can also be an investor's downfall.

Risk: When Bad Things Happen to Good Bonds

A number of factors affect the value of a bond: the state of the economy, supply and demand and the bond issuer's stability. As we said earlier, U.S. Treasuries and savings bonds are the only risk-free securities (if held to maturity). When it comes to all the rest, you have to factor in:

Market risk. If interest rates rise, there may be an overabundance of high-paying bonds, reducing the value of yours. Similarly, there's liquidity risk, meaning you may not be able to sell your bonds if interest rates aren't favorable.

Default risk. This is the risk that the issuer will become insolvent and default on payments.

Inflation risk. If inflation rises, the interest income and the principal you're paid back at maturity will buy less down the road than the same amount today. The longer the term, the greater the risk that inflation might eat away at your returns.

Early call/Reinvestment risk. If the issuer exercises its call option prematurely, you may have to scramble to reinvest your money at attractive rates.

Then there's always the risk of unexpected events that could impact negatively on your investments such as calamities, war, changes in the tax laws, and so on.

It Looks Like a Bond and Acts Like a Bond, but It's a . . .

There are some investments that offer fixed income but aren't debt instruments:

Bank certificates of deposit (CDs) are fairly well known to consumers. They're also called time deposits; you deposit them for a set time period and earn a set rate of interest. Like savings bonds, bank CDs cannot be sold to anyone else. And they can be just as safe as Treasuries; if the financial institution is insured by the Federal Deposit Insurance Corporation (FDIC), your investment is protected up to $100,000. Interest is subject to federal, state, and local tax.

Fixed annuities are contracts between you and an insurer. You give the company a lump sum of money and they give you a fixed stream of payments, for a set period of time or life. There are different

TABLE 2.1   Bonds: The Rating Agencies

Credit Quality	Moody's	S&P	Fitch
Solid as rock	Aaa	AAA	AAA
Very fine quality	Aa1	AA+	AA+
	Aa2	AA	AA
	Aa3	AA–	AA–
Strong capacity to pay	A1	A+	A+
	A2	A	A
	A3	A–	A–
	A	A	A
Adequate ability to pay; lowest investment grade for banks	Baa1	BBB+	BBB+
	Baa2	BBB	BBB
	Baa3	BBB–	BBB
Somewhat speculative; risk exposure	Ba1	BB+	BB+
	Ba2	BB	BB
	Ba3	B–	B–
More speculative; risk exposure	B1	B+	B+
	B2	B	B
	B3	B–	B–
Major risk exposure; on verge of default	Caa1	CCC+	CCC+
	Caa2	CCC	CCC
	Caa3	CCC–	CCC–
Crucial risk exposure; may have defaulted on interest payments	Ca1	CC+	CC+
	Ca2	CC	CC
	Ca3	CC–	CC–
Default or Imminent Default	C	C	C
General default	D	D	D
No rating requested	NR	NR	NR

Source: The Money-Making Guide to Bonds by Hildy Richelson, Bloomberg Press.

types of annuities—immediate or deferred, fixed or variable, for example—and there are many different variations as to tax implications, payment schedules, revocability, fees, interest, and so on. You can find out much more about them at *www.annuityadvantage.com* or *www.annuity.com*.

There are far too many varieties of fixed-income securities to cover in just one chapter. They run the gamut from adjustment bonds to Z-tranches. But with the overview of the major types, you now have a grasp of the fundamentals of fixed-income investing. Now, on to cold, hard cash.

Coach Moglia's Game Plan

1. Compared to stocks, bonds seem boring. *But you need both.* Bonds are less volatile than stocks, and especially good when you're approaching retirement. They can be a great source of steady income over many years, and they usually go up in value when stocks go down, balancing your risk and return.

2. *If safety is your primary concern, consider Treasury bonds, bills and notes.* They are some of the safest investments you can make. They're backed by the U.S. government, but because they offer very low risk, you'll earn lower rates.

3. *Invest in state, local government, and school district bonds to earn tax-free interest.* Those *municipal* and other bonds (munis) can generate a lucrative "real" return when compared to your taxable investments. If you're concerned about your income taxes, munis can pay you steady income and may cut your tax bill, all with relatively low risk.

chapter three
CASH

Cash *n* [Fr. Caisse, a box, money box, cash] **1**: Money that a person actually has, including money on deposit; esp., ready money **2**: Bills and coins; currency **3**: Money, a check, etc. paid at the time of purchase.
Source: Merriam-Webster's Collegiate Dictionary, 11th edition

In the financial world, a cash investment has the following components: *liquidity* and *preservation of principal*. A cash deposit, therefore, is one that is both safe and available. If you can *quickly* turn an investment into funds for spending or investing elsewhere without being penalized either for early withdrawal or from a tax standpoint, you've got cash. And, as they say, cash is king.

If the cash portion of your savings is meant to be an emergency or rainy day fund, it should be completely and almost immediately accessible. After all, if you're laid off, have unexpected medical bills, or any other kind of emergency, there's little comfort in knowing, "well, it's just three more months until that CD comes due." Nor would you want to have to forego the three to six months' interest penalty that comes with early withdrawal.

Let's look at the various options for stashing cash that will have your money earning money, yet will come when you call.

Interest-Bearing Checking Accounts

These accounts only pay an average .25 percent at banks, plus you'll get hit with a fee if your balance dips below the required minimum.[1] If you generally keep hefty sums in your checking account because you draw on that much in the course of the month, you might as well earn a little interest while it's sitting there, so interest-bearing checking makes sense. But don't keep much more than you generally need for ready cash and to pay bills, since checking accounts weren't really meant to be *savings* vehicles. The fluid nature of money in a checking account is somewhat akin to short-term parking at the airport: run in, run out.

Savings Accounts

These are simple, super-safe ways to keep an emergency fund on tap. One type is a passbook savings account, in which a passbook records each deposit and withdrawal, giving you an up-to-date assessment of your current balance. Another choice is a statement savings account in which you receive a quarterly or monthly statement updating your balance, including interest earned.

Up to $100,000 of your money in most banks and saving institutions should be insured by the Federal Deposit Insurance Corporation (FDIC). (Not every financial institution is FDIC-insured, so check to make sure the official sign stating so is displayed at each teller window where deposits are received.) The $100,000 limit covers assets held in different types of ownership, so that individual, joint, retirement, and trust accounts are all insured separately. It's good to have that kind of insurance in case the bank defaults but, while that does happen, it's pretty rare. A greater concern should be the fact that, if you have $100,000 in a bank account earning a pittance, once you factor in cost of living increases and inflation, you may end up losing more money than you earned.

Let's digress for a moment to explain the distinction between the two figures you'll generally see quoted: annual percentage rate (APR) and annual percentage yield (APY). The APR is the amount of interest the bank is paying you to keep your money there. The APY—the actual return—will depend upon the APR and how often the bank pays out interest. Once interest is paid, it is added to the amount in your account and then interest is automatically paid on that new, increased amount.

Through the wondrous power of *compounding*—paying interest on top of reinvested interest payments that are added to your balance—the yield will always be higher than the interest rate. The more frequently interest is paid and the greater the amount on which interest is paid, the higher the ultimate return, or yield. In the savings arena, percentages generally refer to yield, so we'll stick with that.

The current average APY for a savings account is a paltry .49 percent![2] Put another way: You're less than one-half of one percent away from paying the bank to hold onto your money! Of course, as we all know, rates fluctuate; in the early 1990s, savings rates reached over five percent, but by the late 1990s, they hovered around two percent.[3] Even though all signs now indicate that rates are slowly on the rise again, you'll still earn the least in a bank savings account compared to other options.

You'll do a tad better with an account at a "thrift" rather than a traditional commercial bank. Thrifts historically invested depositors' assets in mortgages, and savings and loans once primarily provided home mortgages. Since banks were deregulated in the 1980s, however, these institutions provide many of the same services as other banks. They're averaging .52 percent for a passbook and .58 percent for a statement savings account.[4]

Another variety of thrift is a credit union, a members-only financial institution that will normally top banks' interest rates on savings accounts. Members share a common bond, whether it's an employer, alma mater, union, fraternity or sorority, and so on. Right now, credit unions are paying .73 percent—an improvement, but still nothing to write home about.[5]

When it comes to bank savings accounts, any way you look at it, once you factor in taxes and an annual three percent inflation rate, you're still giving more than you're getting. Even for just a rainy day fund, there are wiser and equally safe places to keep your money.

Money Market Funds

Also called money market mutual funds and money funds, money market funds are a type of mutual fund. So why aren't we waiting to talk about them in the chapter on mutual funds? Good question. It's because money market funds are really a hybrid—they're a cross between savings accounts and mutual funds, with those two key cash components of safety and liquidity.

These funds pool a diverse cross-section of short-term debt instruments and allow an individual investor to buy shares for just $1.00 each. Deposit $1,000 and you'll get 1,000 shares. The net asset value (NAV) of the shares stays fixed at $1.00, although the number of shares will go up as your account grows through additional deposits or accumulation of interest. This is different from non-money mutual funds, where share prices go up and down in response to the open market. Your investment is secure in that sense—as well as another.

Money market fund assets are not FDIC-insured. To my knowledge no individual has ever lost money in these funds, however, it is possible to lose money in a money market fund—the fund seeks to preserve the value of your investment but there are no guarantees. They have never dipped below the $1.00 share price, known as "breaking the buck," in Wall Street parlance. Even in times of default, mutual fund families and parent corporations have backed money funds and their shareholders to hold the share price steady at a dollar. The short-term maturity of money fund investments helps secure against the uncertainty of interest rate fluctuations and market risk. Every investment must mature in less than 13 months and the average maturity of all holdings is no longer than 90 days. The diversification, and lack of long-term debt instruments, equates money funds with relative safety.

Money funds also meet the other criteria of a cash investment: liquidity. Your assets can be redeemed via checkwriting, telephone, mail or wire transfer. Depending on the fund, there may not be a limit to the number of checks you write or redemptions you take, but there will likely be a minimum check amount. Further, investors must incur expense ratios—fees that pay for some of the fund's operating costs. It may only be .60 percent, but it's an expense you would not incur at a bank.[6]

So why would anyone prefer a money fund? Convenience, mostly. Many investors like the idea of having all their money in one place. It's easy to just sweep money out of a money fund with a mouse click or a call and transfer it elsewhere within the same brokerage or investment firm to capitalize on a buying opportunity. You get to skip the step of having to go to a bank and first have the funds transferred to and deposited in your brokerage firm account. Plus, depending on the type of fund, there may be tax advantages.

There are both taxable and tax-exempt money funds. They differ in the investment choices they can make and in the ultimate after-tax earnings you can reap.

Taxable Funds

U.S. Treasury-only. As the name implies, these funds only invest in T-bills, which we already know are backed by Uncle Sam. While your earned interest is taxed on the federal level, in many cases, it may be exempt from state and local taxes.

Government-only. In addition to T-bills, these funds take your money and invest it in Fannie Mae, Sallie Mae, and the other government-sponsored entities we discussed. Because the agencies aren't techni-cally part of the federal government, there's no full faith and credit backing, like there is with T-bills; since the risk is ever so slightly greater, so is the yield.

General-purpose. These are the highest yielding of the money funds. Quiz time: Is risk higher or lower? Right! It's higher, but again, only slightly. These funds invest in short-term corporate loans (called commercial paper), Yankee Dollar CDs (CDs of foreign banks with U.S. branches) and Eurodollar deposits (money in foreign branches of U.S. banks).

Tax-Exempt Money Funds

Like their taxable brethren, these funds invest in short-term debt instru-ments of municipal and state agencies as well as non-profit institu-tions. A caveat: Just like municipal bonds, these funds may trigger the alternative minimum tax if they involve "private activity," so be sure to check the prospectus or ask a customer service representative.

Aside from earnings being exempt from federal taxes, residents of the following states can invest in funds that are also free of state and local taxes: Arizona, California, Connecticut, Florida, Massachusetts, Maryland, Michigan, Minnesota, New Jersey, New York, North Carolina, Ohio, Pennsylvania, Virginia, and Texas.[7]

The yields are lower in tax-exempt funds, but the tax breaks may make this a more profitable choice than taxable funds, depending upon an investor's tax bracket and whether earnings are also exempt from state and local tax. As with municipal bonds, you need to calculate the taxable equivalent yield, that is, the return you would receive with a taxable fund. Only by comparing apples to apples—higher-yield taxable to lower-yield tax-exempt—can you determine which is more beneficial. Here's how:

$$\text{Taxable equivalent yield} = \frac{\text{tax-free yield}}{1 - \text{your marginal federal tax bracket}}$$

So let's say an investor in the 31-percent tax bracket is deciding between a tax-free fund that yields two percent and a taxable fund that yields four percent. Using the above formula, $[2.89 = 2\ /\ (1 - .31)]$, we can see that the after-tax yield is 2.9 percent, so he'll be better off in the taxable fund.

If you're just looking for a place to park liquid savings, there are still other choices we've yet to look at.

Money Market Accounts

There's Army versus Navy. The Dallas Cowboys versus the Washington Redskins. Bill Parcells versus Joe Gibbs. Then there's money funds versus money market accounts (MMAs). While they may not be able to claim the notoriety and fan base of those other rivalries, the competition is just as intense.

Money funds were created in the early 1970s.[8] Regulation prevented a level playing field and banks were unable to compete. The result? Millions of dollars hemorrhaged out of banks and into money funds. Finally, in 1982, deregulation permitted banks to offer competitive rates and the rivalry began in earnest.[9]

Traditional bank MMAs offer higher yields than standard bank savings accounts and generally have higher required initial deposits, but they've yet to best the average APY of money funds. MMAs now average just .55 percent, while money funds average 1.01 percent![10] You're required to maintain a minimum balance and can make up to six withdrawals a month, no more than three via check. One key advantage MMAs have over money funds is that they share the same $100,000-per-type-of-account FDIC protection as savings accounts.

To bump up an MMA's yield, you'll have to boost your balance a few thousand notches and open what is called—no surprise here—a high-yield money market account. The higher the minimum required balance, the higher the yield. And while rates are constantly in flux, the average APY for a high-yield money market with at least $10,000 is currently 1.56 percent and, for $25,000, you'll earn 1.86 percent.[11]

Still not high enough? You'll have to log onto your computer to see where MMAs really shine. Brick-and-mortar banks simply cannot compete with the yields of on-line, or virtual, banks. Here's why: Think of the overhead costs involved in renting, furnishing, lighting, heating and cooling buildings, salaries for tellers, pricey paper transactions, and so on. Sure there are salaries and customer service representatives as well as other expenses at an on-line bank, but it doesn't compare to the cost of maintaining a brick-and-mortar operation.

Here are some top on-line bank picks and their current APYs:[12]

- VirtualBank.com (2.15 percent)
- ING.com (2.10 percent)

- Giantbank.com (2.03 percent)
- Netbank.com (1.7 percent)
- Everbank.com (1.51 percent).

Finally, you can take it even one step higher, with lesser known but high-yielding corporate MMAs. These blue-chips don't invest their—or should we say your—money outside the corporation. Deposits get rolled into the corporation's business. Minimum deposits range from $250 up to $1,000 and rates go up to 2.43 percent. There's General Electric's GE Capital, Caterpillar Money Market, and General Motors' GMAC's Demand Notes (the only one that is affiliated with a bank, so it can offer FDIC protection).[13]

So where does that leave you? You have a lot of things to consider: your needs, what purpose your cash is serving, your tax bracket, your comfort level with the various options, and so on. Any one of them will do the trick when it comes to keeping your rainy day fund safe and available. If you have *extra* cash—more than you would need for monthly bills and three to six months' worth of expenses—your best bet as far as yield is probably an on-line money market account. But if convenience and ease of investing is your top priority, you may very well be better off with a money fund within a brokerage account. No one knows you better than you.

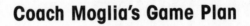

Coach Moglia's Game Plan

1. Savings plans have been paying *painfully* low rates in recent times. Although CDs are at low yields right now, 1- and 2-year CDs are yielding much better than savings accounts.

2. If you're in a higher tax bracket, a tax-exempt money market fund could net you a better return than you'll get with comparable taxable investments. But watch out for the AMT (alternative minimum tax).

chapter four
MUTUAL FUNDS

I n the beginning, there were individual stocks and bonds. Then, in 1924, the first mutual fund was created. Investors saw the product and said that it was good. In fact, it was so good that, after just a year, the fund had $392,000 and 200 shareholders.[1] One fund begat another and today, 80 years later, there are over 8,600 mutual funds in the United States with about $7.54 trillion in assets held by more than 80 million shareholders.[2]

Funds were growing slowly but steadily until the end of the 1970s, when something happened to really make them go "boom!"

Uncle Sam put the *fun* in *fun*ds in 1981 when the government changed the law and provided that at least a portion of retirement plan contributions would be tax-deductible. Guess Congress' TV-obsessed constituents needed some excitement after the "Who Shot J.R.?" furor died down. But I digress...

The funds in 401(k) plans and IRAs took off like wildfire. And they've pretty much ruled the roost when it comes to the average American's savings. One out of two households—more than 80 million people—have invested money in mutual funds, whether inside or outside of a retirement plan.[3]

What's behind Miss Mutual Fund's winning streak in the investment pageant? After all, there are quite a few contestants vying for that tiara. Some years, funds have had stunning returns, while other years, there are plenty of wallflowers. Some are thinly traded, while still others are bloated, overweight, and can't dart about as easily. Let's see whether their beauty is only skin deep, or if they're still deserving of the crown.

Exactly What Are Mutual Funds?

We've already talked about money market funds, the "dollar store" of mutual funds, in which cash and short-term loan investments are pooled and investors buy into the action for a net asset value (NAV) of $1.00 a share. In the rest of the mutual fund world, that is, the stock and bond arenas, the NAV is the total value of a fund's stock divided by the number of shares. It goes up and down and is rarely $1.00 a share. The majority of funds are *actively managed*, meaning they have one, or sometimes two, managers who decide what and when to buy and sell.

Like a money fund, other mutual funds are pools of investments—be they stocks or bonds or a variety of other specialties—that anyone can buy into for a small sum. There's never a shortage of shares, either. If they run out, they can always create more. (One exception is closed-end funds, which have a limited number of shares and trade like a stock, Here, however, we'll stick to open-ended funds, which are the majority).

Funds: Better than Individual Stocks and Bonds?

Of course, there's never one answer for everyone, but in general, investing in a mutual fund is better for *most* people—certainly the average investor—than buying individual equities and bonds. With a mutual fund, you get:

- *Skilled stock and bond pickers.* A portfolio manager has experience in selecting holdings and managing fund assets. When you own individual equities and bonds, you're your own portfolio manager. And if you're like most people, even if you could nail every question in the "Investments" category on *Jeopardy!*, your expertise is probably not on par with that of professional portfolio managers.
- *Instant diversification.* Divvying up your savings among your five or 10 favorite companies isn't going to cushion you sufficiently against a severe market downturn. Equity funds, however, own stock in 173 companies, on average. With a mutual fund, the diversification is done for you, which could help in a downturn.
- *More shares without paying more.* By electing to have dividends and capital gains reinvested automatically, extra shares are purchased and folded into your account.
- *Convenience and simplicity.* If you own a few funds within the same fund family (like Vanguard, T. Rowe Price, INVESCO, and so on), you can switch a portion or all of your savings from one fund to another. No need to fuss with paperwork, waiting for checks to clear, and so on.
- *Liquidity.* Aside from tax considerations, if you want to redeem your investment, simply cash in your shares and you'll be fund-free by the next day. Unlike stocks, mutual fund shares are priced and sales are executed at the market's close, so you would have to wait until the next morning to stash them elsewhere. However, also unlike stocks, you don't have to wait for a broker to find a buyer for your shares. The fund will either resell the shares or buy them itself.
- *Low minimums.* Hundreds of funds lower the minimum required deposits if you sign up for an automatic investment plan (AIP). As little as $50 is electronically deducted from your checking account once or twice a month and swept into the mutual fund.

All That Glitters is Not Gold

There are a few downsides to funds, such as the lack of *transparency.*
If you own individual stocks, you know precisely what you own and
how much you own. Not so with mutual funds. So as not to tip their
hand to competitors, holdings are announced only periodically, usually when it's printed in the annual report, and by then the information may be outdated.

Another negative is *taxes.* When you sell individual equities, you
pay capital gains tax on any profit. A fund sells its holdings throughout the year, generating capital gains tax. But even if you have not
sold your shares, you'll be visited by the phantom Ghost of Taxes
Present and have to fork over money to cover your portion of the
fund's capital gains assessment.

The lack of transparency and the tax implications are incon-
venient and will make April 15 even more unpleasant. But there's
another downside to actively managed mutual funds, one that can so
vastly inhibit the growth of your investment that it warrants a separate discussion.

How Investing in Mutual Funds Can Cost You Money

Whether you call it a fee, a charge or an expense, there is a whole list
of ways that actively managed mutual funds can separate you from
your money. Here are the primary means by which your assets can
be reduced:

- *Load.* Another word for sales commission, typically it's three to
  six percent, but it can run as high as 8.5 percent.[4] If a fund is iden-
  tified with the letter "A" at the end of its name, it's called an A
  share, which means you pay a front-end or up-front load. The
  charge comes straight off the top of your investment. So if you

plunk down $10,000 and there's a five percent front-end load, $500 is deducted and only $9,500 is actually invested. Class A shares will typically have smaller annual 12b-1 fees than class B or class C shares, and discounts on the front end load may be available at certain breakpoints.

B shares have a back-end load, meaning you're charged when you redeem the shares, though some funds phase out the sales charge over time. 12b-1 annual fees are usually higher than for class A shares. C shares have annual fees that are even higher than other classes, so if you're planning to hold the fund for the long term, it's wise to stay away from them.

Additionally, there are many high-performing no-load funds and you may be able to find a no-load alternative that is at least equal to—if not better than—a "loaded" fund.

- *Expense ratio.* This is the fund's operating costs, and it includes management and administrative charges. This fee is a percentage of the fund's net assets and is deducted from your return. Most funds also have what are called 12b-1 fees; these cover the costs of marketing, promotion, and distribution. A fund's 12b-1 fees are included in the expense ratio.
- *Redemption fees* are sometimes charged when you pull out of a fund. It sounds like a back-end load, but in this case, the money goes into the fund as opposed to being added to company profits.
- *Exchange fees.* Some fund families discourage inter-fund transfers by charging a fee. If you're picking a fund family—as opposed to a solitary fund—make sure this isn't the case before you invest. It's just another unnecessary way of separating you from your money.
- *Reinvested dividends fees.* Steer clear of funds that charge you to have dividends rolled back into your account; there are plenty of good funds that won't make you pay to keep your own money!

Before we leave the subject of loads and fees, here's a trivia tidbit. Sometimes the same manager is in charge of two funds: one that is loaded with high-expenses and one that is cheap. Why not go for the bargain, considering that you have the same manager in charge? For example, Bill Gross has an amazing track record as a manager and is at the helm of two intermediate-term bond funds; PIMCO Total Return A, which has a 3.75 percent load and .90 percent expense ratio, and Harbor Bond, which has no load and just a .57 percent expense ratio.[5] Here's another way to look at it: What do you get when you look under the hood of a Lexus? A Toyota. And since you don't drive your mutual fund around, why pay more in fees for the same quality investment?

Stock Funds

The 8,600+ mutual funds come in all shapes, flavors, and sizes. First, let's look at stock funds and examine the variety of ways in which they're characterized. One of the first criteria that defines a fund is its size.

Size

Like stocks, funds are divided into *large, medium* and *small*, according to market capitalization—the number of shares multiplied by the value per share. Large-cap funds have capitalizations of over $15 billion, mid-cap, $2 to $15 billion, and small-cap, less than $2 billion. Size and stability often go hand in hand, so large-cap holdings and funds are generally perceived to be less risky than small-caps.

However, this doesn't mean large funds are the "best" or that you should automatically limit yourself when putting together a portfolio. If a few companies do extremely well, the fund's returns may still be dragged down by the poor performance of a majority, or even a sizeable portion, of its other holdings. Large funds have the ability to move the market, but they're cumbersome and are not able to deftly sidestep trouble at a moment's notice. If a mammoth fund wants to pull out of a position, it has to find enough sellers willing to take on its shares.

Investment Goals and Objectives

Capital appreciation is the increase in a company or a fund's share price. Funds that focus on capital appreciation have to be pretty bold, but there's bold and then there's *really* bold.

Growth funds are all about, well, growth. To fund managers, that means earnings. They're not concerned with a stock's price. An aggressive (momentum) growth fund manager has a one-track mind: He or she looks for stocks that have done well and are expected to do even better (no fallen angels or sob stories here).

The name of the game is earnings and growth rates. Growth funds can have very high growth rates, but you should be wary of anything that seems to good to be true. You'll hear a lot of buzz about the numbers, but may not hear much about profits: think Amazon.com and the other Internet standouts in the late 1990s. Historically, though, growth rates run about 10 percent on average, with about one percent more from value and small cap and about one percent less for growth and large-cap.[6] Let these more reasonable figures be your guide.

But there are less risky shades of growth investing. If you are a more mild-mannered investor who doesn't want an ulcer, look for a fund that seeks companies according to the principle of *growth at a reasonable price* (GARP). These companies may have not met the heart-stopping earnings pace required by aggressive managers.

Unlike their momentum cousins, GARP managers are more moderate and look for companies with slow, steady growth.

Value fund managers have a completely different mentality. They are the bargain-hunters. If there were a discount rack on Wall Street, that's where you'd find them. They look for companies going through rough times—union trouble, a change in consumer tastes, and so on—as long as it's *temporary*.

There are *relative value* managers who look for corporations that are a good value relative to an index, the stocks' historical P/E ratio, others in the industry, or even the market as a whole. *Absolute value* managers just look at the number after the dollar sign. They figure out what they think a company's share price should be and if it's selling for less, they scoop it up. Of course, hopefully, they pay attention to that old caveat: Man—or woman—cannot live by "cheap" alone. Okay, so it's a variation on the old caveat, but you get the point: Just because a stock comes cheap doesn't make it a good buy. A cheap stock may be cheap because it's not worth much. If that's the case, it's no bargain.

So which is better: growth or value? It depends on when—and whom—you ask. The investment world is cyclical and certain pairs usually run counter to one another. Generally speaking, when stocks are up, bonds are down. When growth is soaring (like in the late 1990s tech boom), value is tanking. In fact, just when value investing was on the verge of being completely discredited, the tech boom went bust and, for the next three years, value funds thrived.

If you can't decide between the two and don't want multiple funds, mix it up. That's what *blended funds*, or growth-value hybrids, do. That way, it's easy to keep tabs on what you own and you get to cover all—or at least most—of your bases.

Income funds own companies that make dividend distribution a priority. Investors focused on dividends may simply be more conservative (in which case they may choose to have the dividends reinvested), or they may be retired and rely on dividends to supplement their income. There are also assorted and sundry types of income funds; for example, *growth and income funds* try to find both companies that stress capital appreciation and others that provide investors with income. *Equity-income funds* are mostly made up of blue-chip stocks—old geysers, or established companies. Their prime motivation is to make profits and share it with investors.

We've been addressing United States or domestic equity funds. There are also *international stock funds* (which invest in companies around the world outside the United States) and global stock funds (which buy companies all over the world including those in the United States). (Refer to disclosure in the Foreword.) In addition, there are a number of "specialty" funds: *sector funds* that only own companies in a particular industry, such as oil, utilities, technology, or pharmaceutical companies; *real estate funds* that own pools of investments called real estate investment trusts (REITs); *precious metals funds* that invest in gold, silver, and so on; *bear market funds* that make money when the stock market goes *down;* and many other special types of funds.

Bond Funds

The types of bond funds mirror the kind of individual bonds that we discussed in Chapter 2. To review, they're divided according to length of maturity (when the IOU, or bond, stops earning interest and must be repaid): short-term, intermediate-term, and long-term. The longer the maturity, the higher the risk, since that leaves a greater time period in which one is vulnerable to interest rate fluctuations that alter the price of the bond.

For every type of bond there is a bond fund in which that particular IOU is pooled. The greater the diversification, the more spread out your investments, the lower the risk. There are the federally tax-exempt *muni funds* for state and local government bonds; the same Alternative Minimum Tax (AMT) red alert holds true with funds, so remember to ask whether there's "private activity" in any of the fund's holdings. There are also *corporate bond funds*, government taxable funds, and treasury inflation-protected securities funds (TIPS).

If you only want to have a single fund, and depending on your age and income, look for a stock-bond mix called a *balanced* or *asset allocation fund*. Balanced funds have a fixed proportion of stocks and bonds. With asset allocation funds, the manager has the authority to shift the proportion of stocks and bonds as he or she sees fit, or even liquidate holdings and tuck the money into the cash portion of the fund, depending upon the near-term outlook for the economy and Wall Street.

Index Funds

Index funds track an index, a list of a certain category of companies (or debtors, in the case of bonds) considered to be a representative sampling of that group. Some companies may be weighted more heavily than others, depending upon the index. The granddaddy of all index funds is the Vanguard 500 Index, which tracks the S&P 500. Almost 30 years later, there are 406 stock and bond index funds.[7] Many track the Dow (30 large-cap companies), the Russell 2000 (top mid-caps), the NASDAQ 100 (top tech and biotech companies, among others), and the Wilshire 5000, which tracks the vast majority of stocks that trade on an exchange. There's also the international stock index, the Morgan Stanley Europe, Australia, and Far East (MSAFE). And there are bond indexes as well, such as the Lehman Brothers Government Bond Index and the Lehman Brothers Corporate Bond Index.

What's so great about index funds? Here's what:

- *You may earn more.* Time to 'fess up. Until now, we've been focusing on actively managed funds. Remember when I said that fund managers have a great deal of experience in stock and bond selection? Well, that was the truth. But when it comes down to it, expertise just isn't enough. As often as not, in fact, stock picking can be plain ol' dumb luck.

  In fact, there are numerous studies and mounds of research that show actively managed funds simply cannot beat broad market index returns on any sort of consistent basis. Oh, you'll hear of wizards that have hot streaks and it's true that sometimes they get the selection and the timing just right. (Heck, even a stopped clock is right twice a day.) But the numbers don't lie. Over time, index, or passive, investing trumps active investing. For the past 15 years, the average annual return for actively managed funds was 7.43 percent. During that same time period, index funds reaped 8.63 percent![8]

- *You'll typically get to keep more of what you earn.* The returns you'll usually see quoted—including the ones just mentioned earlier—are returns that are *before-tax* and *exclusive of fees.* Once you factor in the capital gains tax that must be paid each year, your wallet will feel lighter. And don't forget that some active funds have an extremely high rate of turnover. Lots of trading equals high commission costs. A fund that tracks an index, however, only changes its holdings when the index does, and that doesn't happen too often.

Last but certainly not least, there are the fund expenses. As we discussed earlier when we compared funds to individual stocks and bonds, expenses nibble away at your returns and, over time, it's more like a feast! But index funds are a whole other animal. When it comes to expenses, it's a slam-dunk in favor of index funds; they boast a lean, mean average of .82 percent, while actively managed funds have an average expense ratio of 1.55 percent![9]

To see just how much of a difference expenses can make in the growth of an investment, compare Vanguard 500 Index which charges a mere .18 percent to the actively managed ABN AMRO Growth C large-cap growth fund with a weighty 1.88 percent.[10] Let's assume you invested $10,000 and earned a 10 percent average annual return. When less money is deducted from your account to pay expenses, more of it remains to benefit from compounding; the accounts with the higher expenses are losing the benefit of that money, since more is continually being withdrawn. After a 20-year period, the $10,000 in the actively-managed fund would be just $47,656, but in Vanguard, it would have grown to $65,107—a difference of $17,451! And a $100,000 investment would have produced a gap of $174,500! If all managers over time revert to the mean—reflected in an index—why on earth would you pay *more* to earn *less*?

Index funds are not without their limitations. For example, a manager is unable to buy a company that isn't listed on the index, even if he or she feels it's a great prospect. Also, the manager can't take shelter in a storm. If the market gets turbulent, an active-fund manager can shift assets into cash to wait it out. There's nowhere to hide, though, with index funds. Nevertheless, the advantages typically far outweigh the disadvantages. And you'll hear this from investment experts far and wide, from Warren Buffett to John Bogle of Vanguard, and many more.

Ted Aronson swears by index investing. He put his savings into the Vanguard 500 Index fund when it first opened and has watched his money grow at a robust pace. Not only that, all of his money in taxable accounts is invested in 10 other Vanguard index funds. This index fund fanatic's devotion is even more impressive—and surprising—than you realize. That's because Ted is an active *money manager of over $7 billion in institutional money and retirement portfolios. His retirement nest egg is invested in his company's Quaker Small Cap Value Fund: "The fund trades a lot, so it's not suitable for taxable investments. All my taxable money is in Vanguard's index funds."* [11]

Well, there you have it. And Ted is far from alone. Peter Lynch, the revered investment personality and former manager of Fidelity's flagship Magellan Fund, admitted, "Most individual investors would be better off in an index mutual fund." [12] Experts are generally in agreement: Outdoing the indexes is a statistical long shot. Novice and experienced investors alike should accept the power of passive investing and forego the element of chance involved in spotting the next hot pick.

I grant you that hot picks can be a lot more exciting than opting for a passive, ho-hum—even outright boring—index fund. Is there a secret part of you that fantasizes about taking your savings to Las Vegas or Atlantic City and risking it all by throwing the dice, hoping to roll a hard eight? To that I say, take five percent of your money and go a little wild. But let the lion's share ride—safely and cheaply—on an index. Building wealth and keeping what you earn isn't boring. Trust me.

How to Pick a Fund

Before you even think about investing in any fund, it's essential to research it thoroughly. Morningstar.com provides valuable data you need to know; however, be sure to also look at the specific prospectus, and don't hesitate to check other financial research (see Figure 4.1). So don't make a move until you've found and are satisfied with the following information:

- *Investment objective.* What is the fund's goal—growth or income? What is its approach to stock selection? Is the focus on earnings, share price, or both?

- *Past performance.* Yes, we know it's no guarantee of future results, but it's certainly a factor to consider. Has performance been fairly positive and consistent over five or 10 years? Or does the chart showing historical returns look more like the EKG of someone having an anxiety attack? Compare returns to the category or industry average.

- *List of fees.* Look for a fund's expense ratio, redemption fee, and whether it has a load. You can't tell if a fund has a load simply by looking at the name unless it has a letter at the end; if that's the case, it's definitely loaded. However, having a load is not necessarily a deal-breaker. If the returns are so outstanding that they more than make up for the sales charge or you're entitled to breakpoint benefits, don't eliminate the fund from contention. Another thing to remember: Just because a fund is an index fund, don't assume it's a cheap choice. All index funds were not created equal. Vanguard 500 Index's expense ratio is a mere .18 percent, but the Morgan Stanley S&P 500 Index has a .70 percent expense ratio and—get this!—a whopping 5.25 percent load to boot![13]

- *Turnover.* As we said earlier, the potential tax consequences of frequent trading and capital gains can be another return-reducer. Unless you're selecting the fund for a retirement account, look for a turnover ratio in keeping with other similar funds. Of course, it's possible to have a fund that's so outstanding that its returns eclipse its fees. There are no black-and-white rules, but use it as a yardstick to follow for optimum tax efficiency.

M⦶RNINGSTAR.com

Dodge & Cox Stock DODGX

Performance more

Growth of $10,000   12-31-04

		2000	2001	2002	2003	2004
● Fund	16.3	9.3	-10.5	32.3	19.2
● +/- Cat	6.4	12.7	8.0	3.9	6.3
● +/- S&P 500	25.4	21.2	11.6	3.7	8.3

Trailing Returns %   01-14-05

	YTD	3 year	5 year
Fund	-2.20	12.06	11.66
+/- S&P 500	0.06	8.97	14.35

Key Stats more

Morningstar Category	**Morningstar Rating**
Large Value	★★★★★
NAV (01-14-05)	**Day Change**
$127.36	$0.71
Total Assets($mil)	**Expense Ratio %**
41,437	0.54
Front Load %	**Deferred Load %**
None *	None *
Yield % (TTM)	**Min Investment**
1.14	closed

*closed to new investors

Portfolio Analysis more   09-30-04

Morningstar Style Box ❷

Average Mkt Cap $Mil
20,344

Price/Prospective
Earnings
15.7

Asset Allocation % more ▶▶

Cash	3.5
Stocks	96.5
Bonds	0.0
Other	0.0

Annual Turnover %	8
% Assets in Top 10	24.18

Sector Breakdown (% of stocks) ❷

◔ **Information**	**20.22**
🄺 Software	0.78
🄷 Hardware	5.68
🄼 Media	8.21
🄣 Telecommunications	5.55
◑ **Service**	**45.00**
🄷 Healthcare	12.24
🄒 Consumer Services	6.08
🄑 Business Services	8.08
🄢 Financial Services	18.60
🄜 **Manufacturing**	**34.78**
🄒 Consumer Goods	6.93
🄘 Industrial Materials	15.09
🄔 Energy	9.44
🄤 Utilities	3.32

Top 5 Holdings Get Price Quotes

	Sector	YTD Return %	% Net Assets
⊕ Hewlett-Packard*	Hardware	-4.29	2.95 %
⊕ AT&T Wireless Services	Telcommunications	---	2.82 %
⊕ Comcast A*	Media	0.87	2.80 %
⊕ HCA*	Healthcare	8.51	2.43 %
⊕ News Corporation ADR A	Media	---	2.28 %

⊕ Increase ⊖ Decrease ✺ New since last portfolio   * Analyst Report available
YTD Return through 01-14-05.

News, Alerts, and Opinions more

Date	Headline
01-06-05	Manager change (M*)
12-29-04	Fund Dividend Distribution (M*)
12-13-04	Five Finalists for Domestic Manager of the Year (M*)
12-07-04	➠ New Morningstar Analyst Report - Dodge & Cox Stock (M*)
11-18-04	What Makes a Fund an Analyst Pick? (M*)

FIGURE 4.1   **Equity Profile—Provided for Illustrative Purposes Only**

- *Portfolio manager.* Has the manager been there for at least a few years or did he or she just ride into town? If the fund has a record of healthy returns, but the long-standing manager just jumped ship, hold off. Management is too important to let it be an unknown quantity.

We just talked about picking funds and I don't want to seem like a pessimist, but many of the criteria to consider when scouting for a good fund prospect are the flip side of what might be considered trouble signs or red flags in a fund you already own. These aren't mandates to sell, but merely factors to take into account and view as part of the whole picture: Has the fund manager left? Have the fund's peers outperformed it for a year or more? Have fees increased? Or has the fund's objective changed to the point where it no longer meets your needs or matches the degree of risk you bargained for?

On the basis of all that you've read in this chapter, it would seem that index funds are the best of all possible worlds. Well, guess what? There may be something even *better.*

Coach Moglia's Game Plan

1. *Mutual funds instantly diversify your money, and your risk, across dozens—even hundreds of stocks.* They're easy to get into and out of. And they're run by portfolio managers with plenty of investing expertise.

2. *But mutual funds have a downside.* You may pay capital gains taxes on your holdings even as your fund is dropping in value. And, funds may charge you to get into the fund, to stay in, and to get out. Make sure you know what fees you are paying!

3. *Look hard at index funds.* Your fees will be much lower and, historically, the returns have been higher over the long run than most actively managed funds.

chapter five
EXCHANGE-TRADED FUNDS

Recipe for an Exchange-Traded Fund

(serves any number of people)

- Select appetizing stock or bond indexes and/or market segments.
- Separate active fund managers.
- Slice expense ratios in half or more.
- Shred taxes to palatable bite-sized amounts.
- Mix and spice to taste.

Voilà! You have an inexpensive yet nourishing delight that can be served as your holdings' main course or as a satisfying side dish. (Ingredients and portions may be altered any time the exchange "kitchen" is open.)

I wish I could say this was my very own secret recipe for the cheapest and most diverse investment on the market today. Unfortunately, the secret is out—and it wasn't mine. And while many people have heard of the ominous-sounding "Spiders," "VIPER," and so on, the average person still isn't sure what they are and why they very well may be the best investment product since the mutual fund.

In 1987, Nate Most, a commodities broker at the American Stock Exchange, had an epiphany. He realized there was a huge area of securities not trading on an exchange: mutual funds. A meeting with Vanguard's then-head John Bogle alerted Most to the trading costs associated with jumping in and out of funds, so he went back to the drawing board. Eventually, he developed the structure wherein a large block of shares—called a "creation unit"—could be broken up into pieces and sold by institutions to individual investors and traded among one another on the secondary market.[1]

Six years later, the first U.S. exchange-traded fund (ETF), the SPDR 500 Trust, was launched on the American Stock Exchange, or AMEX. Based on the S&P 500 with a formal given name of Standard & Poor's Depository Receipts, it's better known by its nickname, "Spiders."[2] An ETF is a hybrid product that is an investment company that is structured like a fund or trust but trades like a stock, just as Nate Most envisioned it. It holds a large portfolio of underlying securities and is a close corollary or an exact replica of an index, reaping comparable yields and returns.

Other ETFs consist of a small but representative sampling of the securities in the index or group it tracks. Today, there are 160 ETFs with over $160 billion in assets.[3] Their popularity has really soared in recent years, especially in light of the mutual fund industry scandals centering on market timing and after-hours trading. You don't have the same ethics considerations or temptations with passive ETFs. For the most part, it's like having a Global Positioning System in your car *and* using cruise control. Your direction is clear—and you don't even have to step on the gas pedal.

ETFs offer a wide variety of ways to invest in portions of the market according to:

• *Asset class.* ETFs use indexes as benchmarks and there are plenty of them—170 according to Morningstar.[4] The most popular are the large-cap S&P 500, the blue-chip DJIA ("Diamonds" or DIA), the tech-oriented NASDAQ 100 (Cubes or QQQQ), the "total stock market" Wilshire 5000, mid-cap Russell 2000, world-wide Morgan Stanley Capital International (MSCI), and fixed-income Lehman Aggregate Bond, just to name a few.

• *Style.* There is a wide selection of ETFs that specifically target equities specializing in *growth* or *value*, usually in combination with company size. Morningstar has popularized asset-style investing with their Morningstar style boxes, but *style* and *size* investment categories have been used for many decades.

The standard style and size categories are: large-cap growth, large-cap value, mid-cap growth, mid-cap value, small-cap growth, and small-cap value. When creating their style-based ETFs, the first decision an ETF-sponsoring company must make is on whose indexes they want to base their ETF. Barclays Global has three series of style-based ETFs, one using indexes from Frank Russell & Co., one using indexes created by Barra and Standard & Poor, and their newest ETFs using the Morningstar style indexes. State Street has chosen to use the Dow Jones style indexes, while Vanguard has based their ETFs on Morgan Stanley's MSCI indexes.[5]

Although there are slight differences in how Frank Russell, Barra, Dow Jones, Morgan Stanley, and Morningstar create their style indexes, they all share the basic concept of investing styles based on a combination of size and objective.

In addition to the growth and value categories for equities, there are different style categories for bonds: long-term bonds, intermediate bonds, short-term bonds, international, and high-yield (junk) bonds.

• *Regions and countries.* The major indexes track performance of stocks (or bonds) of specific regions and countries such as China, emerging markets, Europe, Global, International, Japan, Latin America, and the Pacific (excluding Japan).

• *Sector.* Industry-specific ETFs include the areas of financial services, health/biotechnology, natural resources, real estate, science/ technology, specialty/miscellaneous, telecommunication, and utilities.

Structure of ETFs

An ETF is created when a large institutional investor deposits securities into the fund in return for "creation units" of 50,000-share lots. The shares are then traded and priced on the secondary market, mostly on the American Stock Exchange, but also on the New York Stock Exchange.

Most ETFs are structured as *open-end index mutual funds* (Select Sector Spiders, iShares) or *unit investment trusts*, where a fund manager preselects a portfolio of securities that remains unchanged (Qubes, Diamonds, S&P 500 Spiders). Vanguard created a third structure, which is really a share class. Its Vanguard Index Participation Equity Fund, or Vipers (the ETF honchos just love those cutesy nicknames!) tracks the Vanguard Total Stock Market Index Fund, which in turn tracks the Wilshire 5000.

Finally, there's a *grantor trust*, which is considered a quasi-ETF. However, it doesn't track an index, it is never rebalanced, and the shareholders are considered owners of the underlying securities. Merrill Lynch has a line of these called Holding Company Depository Receipts, or HOLDR funds, in which a group of sector-specific stocks are selected. Since HOLDRs veer so far from the classic ETF mold, however, we won't focus on them.

The majority of ETFs now available are managed by Barclays Global Investors and State Street Global Advisors.

As you'll see, ETFs have almost all of the advantages of index mutual funds—and *then* some:

• *Diversity.* ETFs can serve as a core portfolio or they can flesh out an area in which you're underinvested. They give you not one bite, but an entire smorgasbord of security delights. Lacking in large-cap? There are Spiders, iShares S&P 500, and the Vanguard S&P 500. Need exposure to the international or global markets? With a single pick, you have a representative sampling of the best of that segment of the market.

One of the commandments of investing is to not put all your eggs in one basket (more on that in Chapter 8). With a portfolio of large-cap, small-cap, sector, and global ETFs, you've got an egg in a number of baskets; more precisely, you have a basket of securities in a number of baskets. Market risk is drastically reduced and asset allocation is immediate.

• *Low-cost.* Think about it. They're based on an index, market segment, or preselected grouping. For the most part, there aren't ongoing extensive research costs and there's also no active fund manager to richly compensate for his or her expert stock-picking, stock-dropping, and stock-shuffling. There are no loads and no 12b-1 fees. ETFs' expense ratio averages .60 percent, compared to 1.55 percent for active mutual funds (.82 percent for index funds).[6] Furthermore, since ETFs trade on an exchange, they don't have internal transaction costs for the trades necessary to carry out shareholder purchases and redemptions, as is the case with mutual funds. (See Figures 5.1a, b, and c.)

• *Trading flexibility. You can price and trade ETFs throughout the day*, as opposed to a mutual fund, where a trade can only be executed at the price and time of the market's close. Intraday pricing allows ETFs to be bought or sold at specific price points, so you can utilize stop or limit orders with them—as well as trade on margin—just as with a stock.

• *You can even sell ETFs short on a downtick*, or succeeding downward price movements. In order to sell common stocks short, you

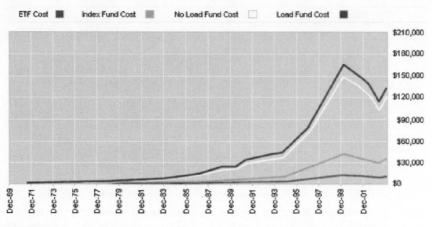

ETF Cost ■   Index Fund Cost ■   No Load Fund Cost □   Load Fund Cost ■

FIGURE 5.1a   Cumulative Cost of Fees and Loads (12/31/69 to 8/31/03).
Source: Ameritrade

The following assumptions were used in constructing this hypothetical:
- The beginning investment on December 31, 1969 is $10,000.
- The time period covered is December 31, 1969 to August 31, 2003.
- Each investment's return is assumed to have the same annual return as the S&P 500 index **before fees** are included.
- The annual expense ratio for each investment is subtracted from the return of the S&P 500 index each year.
- The expense ratio includes management, shareholder servicing, and 12b-1 fees, but does not include commission fees.
- It is assumed the front-end load is withdrawn from the initial investment on December 31, 1969. The beginning value for the front-end load actively managed fund is $9,425.
- The expense ratios used are typical for the average fund in that particular investment category and do not reflect any specific fund family.

must wait for a plus or uptick before the price falls again. The rationale is that with a singular security, the consequences of short-selling gaining momentum and resulting in a downward spiral could be calamitous. ETFs, however, have so many underlying securities that such consequences would be so diluted as to be negligible. The significant risks to an individual investor associated with short selling, as discussed in Chapter 1, remain.

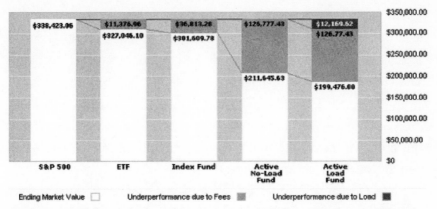

FIGURE 5.1b   Ending Market Values of each Hypothetical Investment (8/31/03).
Source: Ameritrade

• *Transparency.* Unlike actively managed funds, and even many index funds, you can see exactly what holdings are in an ETF at the end of the trading day. You'll know the value of each security and the exact current value of an ETF share, up to and including that day's trading.

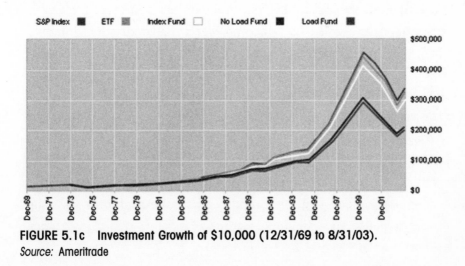

FIGURE 5.1c   Investment Growth of $10,000 (12/31/69 to 8/31/03).
Source: Ameritrade

- *Tax efficiency.* Like index funds, there is low turnover in ETFs, since the sale of an underlying security only takes place when the index is occasionally reconstituted. And again, since ETF investors trade with others on an exchange, any shares they sell don't require the fund to sell securities to generate cash for those shareholders, while possibly generating capital gains to remaining investors. You will, however, have to pay tax on any capital gains that may result from the sale of your own shares.

Suze Orman, the financial phenom and author of seven books, including *The Road to Wealth: Suze Orman's Complete Guide to Your Money*, calls ETFs the "mutual funds for the twenty-first century." Characteristically, she isn't shy about making her preference known: "Those of you who make investments outside of any retirement accounts are absolutely crazy if you are using actively managed funds rather than ETFs, which are designed *not* to make capital gains distributions."[7]

Fixed-income ETFs don't enjoy the same degree of tax efficiency as equity ETFs. As bonds mature, they're eliminated from the index, resulting in higher turnover—and capital gains—than stock indexes. Nevertheless, there's still far less turnover—and, as a result, fewer tax consequences—with fixed-income ETFs than individual bonds or even bond mutual funds.

ETFs are a smart move if:

- *You have a lump sum to invest.* That way, you're paying a brokerage commission just once.
- *You're a buy-and-hold investor* who intends to let his or her investment ride at the cheapest possible price.
- *You're an active trader* who likes the flexibility of trading individual shares and wants to be able to trade throughout the day.

All things considered, experts generally agree that ETFs have it over index mutual funds. Paul Farrell, columnist for CBS Marketwatch. com and author of *The Lazy Person's Guide to Investing* is a passive investing devotee. He feels ETFs are "the perfect solution, a switch-hitting portfolio. You get both a boring, conservative, low-cost, long-term, buy-and-hold portfolio—plus the total flexibility of having fun playing in the stock market whenever you choose. How? By building an all-ETF indexed portfolio. That's right, buy nothing but exchange-traded funds, 100 percent ETFs."[8]

Even so, of course, ETFs may not be right for everyone. ETF downsides are:

- *Dollar-cost averaging* will cost you if you simply don't have a pot of dough to plunk down and are interested in making monthly deposits through an automatic investment plan. Experts generally agree that an index fund is a better choice in that case. The reason? Every time you buy ETF shares, you have to pay the brokerage commission. By making monthly or bimonthly purchases, you'll be exchanging expense ratio savings for trading commission costs, a counterproductive strategy.

- *Market pricing*. The share price is determined by the forces of supply and demand on the secondary market, not the underlying net asset value as with a mutual fund. Investors may end up purchasing shares at a premium or discount to their net asset value. There's also market risk which takes into account changing interest rates and price fluctuations, as well as economic conditions and global events.

- *Tracking error*. An ETF typically pays out dividends received from the underlying stocks on a quarterly basis. However, the under-lying stocks pay dividends throughout the quarter. Therefore, these funds may have a "dividend cash drag," where they hold cash prior to distributing it, even though the underlying index isn't composed of cash. This is one reason that ETFs are not flawless replicas of indexes.

• *Credit risk* is the same as with individual bonds and involves the possibility that a debtor may default or simply delay payments of principal and interest.

• *Interest rate risk* is another risk associated with bonds, since we know that rising rates make bond prices fall. Bonds with longer maturities are especially affected, as are the ETFs that hold them.

On balance, however, to end as I began, ETFs are an inexpensive, effective way to achieve diversification and instant asset allocation: the two keys to unlocking your financial goals and the subject we'll address next.

Coach Moglia's Game Plan

1. *ETFs diversify your money over even more stocks* than the average mutual fund—and you'll pay a fraction of the fees of an actively-managed fund.

2. *Like index funds, ETFs track the market.* Plenty of research has shown that such investments actually outperform most of the more expensive, actively-managed funds.

3. Even though ETFs aren't widely known and understood by the average investor, they could well be *the right choice for your long-term lump sum investment dollars.* The difference in your annual cost may seem small, but ETFs could put tens of thousands of dollars more in your pocket over time.

PART TWO
The Fundamental Principles of Investing

HALF-TIME REPORT

L et's evaluate where we are at this point. In the first half of the book, we talked about the primary asset classes and how they differ. Now, in the second half, we'll see how the distinct pieces of the investment puzzle come together to form a cohesive and complete picture. I'll take you through the five-step process that will teach you how to apply what you know in the most productive, efficient way possible.

Step 1: You'll need to pinpoint your investment goals: Why are you saving, when will you need the money and what's the best vehicle to save for a particular goal?

Step 2: This is the "stop and think" step, where you need to look inward and ask yourself some tough questions about just how much risk you can tolerate without becoming a sleepless nervous wreck. Once you've zeroed in on how much uncertainty you can endure, you can move on.

Step 3: Asset allocation, or how you divvy up your portfolio among the different asset classes and types of investments *within* those classes, is almost universally considered the single greatest determining factor in how well your portfolio performs.

Step 4: We explore the reality that one cannot merely develop a plan, set it on "automatic," and forget about it. Investments do not remain constant, nor would we want them to! However stocks and bonds perform, the portion of your portfolio represented by each will at some point be out of whack. For example, if you want a portfolio that's 80 percent stocks, after a wonderful year for equities, it's likely you're overweighted in stocks. You need to monitor and rebalance, so you're back on course in just the right amounts.

Step 5: We delve into the practicalities of putting a plan into action, such as the different brokerage options for maintaining investment accounts and executing trades.

chapter six
GOALS

You're in the NFL. It's game time. You run out of the tunnel and onto the field, all pumped up by the glare of the lights and the roar of the crowd. But wait. There's a problem. You suddenly realize you're not in uniform, you have no equipment and, worst of all, you have only a vague notion as to the rules of the game. Is this merely a bad dream from which you bound up in bed, drenched in perspiration?

As impossible as it is to fathom, millions of Americans approach their financial destiny the same way as in the imaginary football scenario above. But the lesson in both cases is the same: Just showing up isn't enough. You've got to familiarize yourself with—if not master—the fundamentals, make sure you possess the correct tools, and, most important of all, have a plan. As the saying goes, "Failing to plan is planning to fail." A person facing the future without a plan is like a coach without a playbook: lost, anxious, and at the mercy of fate.

Before you can even think about how to structure and apportion your investments, you have to determine your goals—why you're saving—and your time frame, or when you'll need the money. Setting goals is the very first step in making investment plans for you and your family's future. Now that we have established that having a plan is crucial, let's look at what your different goals might be. And keep in mind that you may have more than one goal at a time.

Retirement

This is the Super Bowl of savings. A recent survey showed that 58 percent of Americans are saving for retirement.[1] Clearly, it's a top priority. Unlike a vacation home or a transatlantic crossing on the Queen Elizabeth II, being able to afford to live comfortably once you retire is essential. You want your money to outlive you, not necessarily to leave large trust funds for the grandkids (although that's nice). You don't want to cut it so close that you end up spending your last dollar on your last day.

And if you wait until you get your gold watch to start saving—do they still give out gold watches?—you're going to be sacked. Famed football coach Vince Lombardi once said, "We didn't lose the game; we just ran out of time." When it comes to saving and investing, however, if you run out of time before you've achieved your goals, you *do* lose the game. Don't let that happen to you.

In case you're wondering why retirement comes before college tuition in the savings hierarchy, it's because, *at the very least*, it's crucial to be able to afford the basic necessities of life (not to mention a few luxuries) once you're no longer bringing home a paycheck. College, while very important to future earnings success, as well as a helluva lot of fun, doesn't garner first-place savings status. Don't get me wrong: Investing in your kids' future is important so they can be independent. Of course, you want them to come home for the holidays, but returning to the roost full-time is another matter. After all, you probably will have just finished turning their bedrooms into a media room, library, or den and it would be a shame to have to undo all that. It's really best for them to be out of the house—I mean, standing on their own two feet.

But seriously, the reason that retirement comes first as far as savings priority is there are plenty of other ways to pay for a diploma *aside* from your savings. With retirement, however, it's *largely,* but thankfully not exclusively, up to you.

How Much Money Will You Need during Retirement?

Of course, there's no way to know precisely, but there are ways to estimate. The rule of thumb is that you'll need about 70 to 80 percent of your current income to live comfortably in retirement. Presumably, some of your expenses should be reduced or eliminated once the kids are grown and the mortgage is paid off. Even so, your earned income will likely be greatly reduced or even eliminated and your savings may shrink due to:

- *Inflation,* which diminishes the buying power of your savings to the tune of roughly three percent a year.
- *Taxes,* which can greatly reduce the amount you've saved once you start making withdrawals, depending upon the type of account in which your money is stashed.

To get a ballpark estimate of how much you'll need, take a few minutes to plug in figures on a retirement calculator at *www. choosetosave.org* (see Figure 6.1).

Other factors that could increase the need for extra savings are:

- *Aging parents*, who may require supplemental financial contributions from you to cover nonreimbursable medical costs.
- *Longer life expectancies* mean that you and your spouse can reasonably expect to live much longer than your parents. The average healthy 50-year-old man and woman can expect to live another 28 and 32 years, respectively.[2] This means you may have to save much more than you originally anticipated.

Planning for retirement is not a one-size-fits-all exercise. The purpose of Ballpark is simply to give you a basic idea of the savings you'll need when you retire.

So let's play ball!

If you are married, you and your spouse should each fill out your own Ballpark Estimate worksheet taking your marital status into account when entering your Social Security benefit in number 2 below.

1. How much annual income will you want in retirement? (Figure at least 70% of your current annual gross income just to maintain your current standard of living. Really.)

Enter your current annual gross income

[80000]

Click on the percentage of your current annual gross income you would like to use as your goal

[56000]

Tips to help you select a goal:

- 70% to 80% - You will need to pay for the basics in retirement, but you won't have to pay many medical expenses. You're planning for a comfortable retirement without much travel. You are older and/or in your prime earning years.
- 80% to 90% - You will need to pay for some medical costs above Medicare, which on average covers about 55%. You plan to take some small trips, and you know that you will need to continue saving some money.
- 100% to 120% - You will need to cover all costs above Medicare. You are very young and/or your prime earning years are ahead of you. You would like a retirement lifestyle that is more than comfortable. You need to save for the possibility of Long Term Care, and you know based upon family history that you may live past 95.

2. Enter the income you expect to receive annually from:

- Social Security

If you make under $25,000, enter $8,000; between $25,000 - $40,000, enter $12,000; over $40,000, enter $14,500 (For married couples - the lower earning spouse should enter either their own benefit based on their income or 50% of the higher earning spouse's benefit, whichever is higher.)   [14500]
For a more personalized estimate, enter the appropriate benefit figure from your Social Security statement from the Social Security Administration (1-800-772-1213, www.ssa.gov). Ballpark assumes you will begin receiving Social Security Benefits at age 65, however the age for full benefits is rising to 67. Your Social Security statement will provide a personalized benefit estimate based on your actual earning history.

- Traditional Employer Pension -- a plan that pays a set dollar amount for life, where the dollar amount depends on salary and years of service (in today's dollars)   [0]

- Part-time income   [0]

- Other   [0]

This is how much you need to make up for each retirement year: [41500]

Now you want a ballpark estimate of how much money you'll need in the bank the day you retire. So the accountants went to work and devised a simple formula. For the record, they figure you'll realize a constant real rate of return of 3% after inflation, you'll live to age 87, and you'll begin to receive income from Social Security at age 65. If you anticipate living longer than age 87 or earning less than a 3% real rate of return on your savings, you'll want to consider using a higher percentage of your current annual gross income as a goal on line 1.

3. To determine the amount you'll need to save, click on the age at which you expect to retire.

55	60
65	70

564400

> **Important Note -** If you want to try different scenerios with Ballpark, clear the worksheet each time and start again. Changing numbers in one part of the worksheet **will not** prompt the rest of the worksheet to recalculate based on the new information. To clear the worksheet, click on the "Clear Form" button at the bottom of the worksheet.

4. If you expect to retire before age 65, click on the age at which you expect to retire.
(Note: This field relates to Social Security and will remain 0 if you entered 0 as your Social Security benefit on line 2.)

55	60

0

5. Enter your savings to date (include money accumulated in a 401(K), IRA, or similar retirement plan as well as money accumulated in savings accounts, savings bonds, certificates of deposit, and other savings vehicles):

250000

Click on the number of years you have until retirement.
What if I have less than 10 years until retirement?

10	15
20	25
30	35
40	

400000

Total additional savings needed at retirement: 164400

Don't panic. Those same accountants devised another formula to show you how much to save each year in order to reach your goal amount. They factor in compounding. That's where your money not only makes interest, your interest starts making interest as well, creating a snowball effect.

6. To determine the ANNUAL amount you'll need to save, click on the button that shows how many years you have until retirement.
What If I have less than 10 years until retirement?
My result is a negative number. What does that mean?

10	15
20	25
30	35
40	

8548

See? It's not impossible or even particularly painful. It just takes planning. And the sooner you start, the better off you'll be.

FIGURE 6.1   Ballpark Estimate

How much will Uncle Sam contribute in your golden years? Not nearly enough. Social Security—sometimes nicknamed Social *In*security, in light of its questionable future—provides a minimal supplement to the monthly income flow. Millions who rely primarily on Uncle Sam to take care of them in retirement find themselves struggling near or below poverty levels. Think of it as a monthly bonus, not the core of your income.

Carefully review your annual earnings statement from the Social Security Administration to make sure the information is accurate. That's the data that's going to determine the amount of Social Security you'll receive, along with the age at which you retire and start collecting benefits.

In order to help you estimate your future benefits, go to *www.ssa.gov* and find out your full retirement age (FRA), the point at which you can expect to receive full benefits. If you were born in 1950, for example, your FRA is 66. Waiting an extra year or two to retire can mean a few hundred extra dollars in each month's check—something worth thinking about. You'll see a scary shortfall between how much you'll need to live comfortably and the amount of your Social Security check. So how do you close the gap? That's where your savings comes into play!

Employer-Sponsored Plans

Uncle Sam has given you gifts to save for your senior years through a variety of special retirement plans. These are the best routes for saving, since you never look a federal gift horse in the mouth.

• *Defined benefit plans* generally refer to what's thought of as the traditional pension plan. A fixed amount is set aside by an employer to provide post-retirement income for the employees who worked at that company for most, if not all, of their careers. The longer the employee has worked for the company, the greater the pension.

• *Defined-contribution plans* are very popular. Quite often they are partially funded by the employee as well as by the employer in the form of matching contributions. The most common type of defined contribution plan is a 401(k); they're also known as 403(b) if the employer is a nonprofit corporation or a 457 plan for state and municipal workers. A percentage of your salary—the average contribution is seven percent—is deducted from your gross pay, thereby lowering the amount of your taxable income, and allowing your retirement fund to grow on a tax-deferred basis.[3] It's pretty foolish not to participate in one of these plans, particularly where an employer matches contributions. The way I look at it: Why would anyone turn down free money?

The plan is administered by an investment company and usually offers about 17 options, including a number of types of mutual funds (stock, bond, and balanced), and a 401(k)-type money market called a stable value fund.[4] Some offer ETFs and other choices as well, while a minority of plans, called "self-directed," allow for complete freedom to invest in whatever the employee chooses.

SEP-IRA or Keogh

A SEP (Simplified Employee Pension Plan) and Keogh are retirement savings vehicles, especially for the self-employed or owners of small businesses. This year, you can contribute as much as $41,000 or up to 25 percent of your income (whichever is less) to a SEP. A small business owner must make employee contributions comparable to his or her own. There are advantages and limitations to each. Another option is a Keogh and it comes in many flavors: profit-sharing, money-purchase plans, and so on. However, Keoghs have full tax-reporting requirements and involve a lot of paperwork; they're probably best for those who want to shelter over $41,000 per year. If you're self-employed or a small business owner, it's best to discuss your options with an accountant.

IRAs

Individual Retirement Accounts (IRAs) have been around over 20 years and have helped many people without employer-assisted plans to save for retirement.

With a *traditional IRA*, you get to contribute—and deduct—up to $3,000 annually from your taxes and it will grow on a tax-deferred basis. (Contributions are set to go up to $4,000 in 2005 and $5,000 in 2008.) Non-working spouses can contribute an additional $3,000 a year into any type of IRA account. There's also a special "catch-up" contribution you can make to an IRA, which aims to help taxpayers 50 years and older speed up the savings; they're now allowed to contribute $3,500 per year.

When you withdraw the money at retirement, you will then have to pay the piper—in this case, Uncle Sam. Withdraw money before you're 59½ and you'll get hit with a 10 percent penalty, too. And even if you don't need the money, the rules require that you start making withdrawals at 70½. If you participate in a 401(k) or other employer-assisted plan where before-tax contributions are made, you can't benefit twice by deducting a contribution to a traditional IRA—that's double-dipping!

Roth IRAs are IRA accounts in which contributions are not tax-deductible, however, when you start withdrawing money, you get all the earnings free of federal tax. Consider a Roth if you don't absolutely need the yearly tax deduction for your contribution and you fall within the income limits: $110,000 (adjusted gross income) for a single, and $160,000 for those who are married filing jointly.

If you have a traditional IRA, should you "convert" to a Roth? You'll end up with more money in your pocket at retirement, so it's a good idea as long as you're eligible and can afford to pay Uncle Sam, since you'll owe tax on the entire converted amount.

A nice touch: Even if you contribute to a 401(k) or other plan with before-tax contributions, you can still fund a Roth. As an aside, if you have other sources of income and don't need to make withdrawals from your Roth, you never have to!

A Roth 401(k) is coming out in 2006 and it appears to be the best of all possible worlds. Contributions won't be deductible, but you'll have the benefit of an employer match, and it will *all* be federal tax-free at retirement!

College Costs

Once you've begun to ensure that your and your spouse's future is secure, you can start to invest in the future of your children. And by that I mean their education.

Traditional Investment Account

You can, of course, simply open an account and start investing. If you opt to go this route, you'll need to decide whether to save in your own name or make it a custodial account and save in your child's name. Up until a child is 14 years old, a limited amount of investment income is taxed at the parents' rate. After age 14, however, it may be a good idea to fund an account in your child's name instead of yours since he or she is undoubtedly in a lower tax bracket—unless your child is Mary Kate or Ashley Olsen, of course.

However, if you think you'll be applying for financial aid, it's a better idea to save in your own name. Colleges expect a child to kick in 35 percent of his or her own assets, but only expect a contribution of up to 5.65 percent of parents' assets.[5] Another reason to save in your own name is that if you don't, once your little one turns 18, the money is hers, so if she should decide to hit the road and do some soul-searching instead of going to college, she can take the money and run!

When it comes to savings for college, there are far better, "tax-smart" options than going it alone.

529 Plans

529 plans are so named for that portion of the Internal Revenue Code that covers these special college accounts. Earnings grow on a tax-deferred basis and withdrawals are exempt from federal tax as long as the money used is for education. Some states also allow contributions to be tax-deductible and earnings to grow tax-deferred. There are two types of 529 plans.

First, there's a *savings program*, where you sign on with a particular state (it doesn't have to be your own) and one of its investment plans, managed by the state's treasurer's office or an investment company. Typically, a plan starts out heavily weighted with stocks and then escalates the more conservative fixed-income portion as the student nears college age.

A recent addition to the list of plans is an Independent 529, administered by Teachers Insurance and Annuity Association of America–College Retirement Equities Fund (TIAA-CREF), in which you can apply your savings to the tuition of a number of private schools. To see a complete listing of 529 savings plans, including all the relevant details as well as rankings, log onto *www.savingforcollege.com* or *www.collegesaving.org*.

A final point on 529 savings programs: Be on the lookout for relationship offers that can help fund your 529 plans. Check out *www.upromise.com* for all sorts of financial product offers.

The second type of 529 plan is called a *prepaid program*, where you contract to lock in tomorrow's tuition at today's prices. By enrolling when your child is young, you could end up getting a college education for half-price.

There are a few drawbacks, however:

- This only pays for an education at one of your state's colleges or universities. If Junior decides he wants to attend a private college or an out-of-state school, you'll get to transfer the money in your account, but will have to pay the difference between your savings and whatever the tuition is at that time.
- If the plan's investments take a dive, the state may close the plan or even raise tuition prices. Check to see if the state's treasury guarantees the plan. During the bear market that started with the tech bubble burst in March of 2000, a handful of states closed enrollments to their tuition prepaid plans.[6]
- Assets in prepaid accounts are considered an outside resource for your child, akin to scholarship money, so it will reduce any financial aid on a dollar-for-dollar basis.

Coverdell Education Savings Accounts

Formerly called Education IRAs, these accounts allow you to contribute up to $2,000 per year. Earnings are tax-free and you don't pay tax on contributions until the funds are withdrawn. Even then you only pay at the child's (lower) rate. However, the money is considered the child's for financial aid purposes and it will reduce any awards. You get to control how and where the account is invested.

Other Payment Options

- Pay tuition with zero percent financing by signing up for a payment plan where you make installment payments over a 10-month period for the full college costs (minus financial aid). Two companies that contract with colleges are Tuition Management Systems (*www.afford.com*; 800-722-4867) or Academic Management Services (*www.amsweb.com*; 800-635-0120). This method still requires being able to swing an extra $1,000 or more a month.

• You could always put the tab on the house, by drawing on a home equity line. The savings aren't tax-free as with a 529, and you'll have to pay interest, of course, but at least the interest is tax-deductible.

• There are special borrowing options for parents, called Parent Loan for Undergraduate Students (PLUS) loans, which have no income requirements and give you 10 years to pay off the loan. Finally, there are a number of financial aid options for students, such as loans, grants, and work-study programs.

Lifestyle Goals

Of course, there are *other* goals to save for, aside from retirement and your children's education, such as a second home, a new car, or extravagant vacations. And let's not forget about plain old wealth accumulation, whether it's simply your desire to have more money or, perhaps, the ability to pass it down to your children or grandchildren.

Unfortunately, unlike retirement savings vehicles, Uncle Sam isn't going to help you out with these goals, so you're on your own. The fastest and safest way to build up your luxury kitty is to set up an automatic investment plan to have as much as you can spare electronically withdrawn from each paycheck and deposited in a mutual fund of your choice. All these goals are obtainable if you set your savings on "automatic" and give yourself a few years to grab that brass ring.

If you're saying to yourself, "I don't have any extra money to put away for retirement, college or anything else—my paycheck just covers my expenses," my response is, "Oh, yes, you do!" There have been mounds of books written just on the subject of budgeting and how to trim expenses. We can't go into it here in great detail, but I can get you started with these five simple ways to find thousands of dollars you didn't even know you had:

1. *Mortgage.* This is most people's biggest fixed expense. Are you paying the lowest possible mortgage rates? On a 30-year, $150,000 loan, paying 5.90 percent instead of 9.29 percent can mean $349 more in your pocket each month! You can save even more with a 15-year mortgage instead of a 30-year mortgage. Find out the best deals at *www.LendingTree.com* and *www. eLoan.com.*

2. *Credit card debt.* The average U.S. household carries $9,205 in plastic debt. Most folks don't even know the interest rate they're paying. Find out. Then log onto *www.CardWeb.com* or *www.CardRatings.com* and see the best, rock-bottom offers around. Transfer balances to a card with a zero percent introductory rate and a low permanent rate.

3. *Phone bills.* These include local, regional, long distance, and cellular calls. Make sure you have the cheapest, most cost-effective plan for your family. Log onto *www.lowermybills.com* to compare rates.

4. *Insurance.* A study by Progressive showed that premiums vary by an average of $524 for insurance offered by different insurers in the same vicinity providing identical coverage. So do just a bit of comparison shopping on *www.Insure.com* or *www. Quotesmith.com.*[7]

5. *Know the score.* All interest rates and insurance premiums can be drastically increased, depending upon your credit score. Get a copy of your credit report and score at *www.myFICO.com* to

make sure the data is current and accurate. A few more points could save you thousands in credit card and mortgage interest rates, as well as all of your insurance premiums. On *MyFICO.com*, it shows that a credit score of 559 instead of 720 can mean a difference of 3.7 percent on a mortgage rate! And if you think your score could never be that low, think again; a recent study showed that a single late payment could drop your score by nearly 100 points![8]

Once you've taken these steps, I can practically guarantee you'll be flush with "extra" money to help at least your most important dreams come true.

Coach Moglia's Game Plan

1. *You can't meet your goals unless you have a plan.* Draw up a list of your goals and then do some number-crunching. Save as much as you can each month and select the savings vehicles that best suits you and your plan.

2. *Make savings for retirement a priority since,* unlike. other goals, it's probably your most essential one. Make sure you have enough money to live comfortably for at least 20 years after you retire.

3. *Never turn down free money.* Always contribute at least enough to meet your employer's match in your 401(k) plan. Once you've met the match, fund a Roth IRA if you meet the requirements.

chapter seven

RISK TOLERANCE

This above all: to thine own self be true.
—William Shakespeare, *Hamlet*

Know thy self.
—Socrates

You may be thinking, "What do those guys know about investing?" No, I'm not having a senior moment and haven't suddenly forgotten the subject of this book. Truth be told, investing can be an emotional, even personal, experience. I don't want to get all touchy-feely here, but before you can begin putting together a portfolio of investments for your different goals, you need to get in touch with your "inner investor." A little soul-searching is in order—nothing major, just a few minutes—so you can determine how much *risk* you can comfortably tolerate. Your risk tolerance affects the investments you choose, which, in turn, directly impacts your approximate anticipated return.

No Pain, No Gain / No Risk, No Return

If someone approaches you with an investment opportunity that boasts a no-risk, guaranteed big-money return, run—do not walk—in the opposite direction. Life, investing, sports—no matter the venue—simply doesn't work that way. In sports, the tougher the opponent, the sweeter the victory. It's the same idea in the world of investing. The greater the risk, the sweeter—or greater—the potential reward. That's why long-shot racehorses pay the most, compared with the favorite going off at only 2 to 1 odds. Basically, the investor who is willing to accept a greater chance that hoped-for returns may *not* be forthcoming will be more richly compensated if those returns are, in fact, realized.

Risk has two basic components: *uncertainty* (that you may never see the sweet reward you'd hoped to see) and *volatility* (that there will be wide swings in both positive and negative directions before you'll need the money).

The more uncertain and volatile the returns, the greater the risk and the more antacid you may need to take. The stock market can be nauseatingly turbulent at certain points, but history shows that bear markets don't last forever. Even so, a lot of people simply don't have the stomach for the roller-coaster ups and downs that can take place.

Of course, the average investor may not be made of the same stuff as professionals like Duncan Richardson, manager of the Eaton Vance Tax-Managed Growth Fund, who says: "There is nothing wrong with volatility unless you become a victim of it. Volatility is the absolute friend of patient investors. We view volatility as creating opportunities. It's great if there is an overreaction to an event, and we can step in and buy stocks for lower prices."[1]

You don't have to get excited by the bumps, like Richardson and other seasoned pros, but if you can withstand them, you'll be glad you did: Stocks invariably trend upward over time. The average annual return of the S&P 500 for the past 25 years is 13.32 percent and 9.97 percent for the past 50 years—an incredibly impressive long-term record.[2]

Remember: Nothing is 100% foolproof. Anytime you pull your money out from under your mattress and deposit it elsewhere, you're taking a chance. What may not be obvious, though, is that you're taking an even *greater* risk by letting it lie dormant in your seemingly secure bedroom.

Types of Risk

As we discussed in Chapter 2, there are many different kinds of risk. Some are specific to bonds, like *default risk*, but most cross all asset class borders. *Market* and *event risk*, caused by economic and political factors—such as recession, war, inflation, deflation, and so on—most definitely have the potential to deplete your savings.

Then there's *investment* or *asset risk*. Stocks aren't inherently high-risk any more than bonds are inherently risk-free. However, *in general*, stocks are considered riskier than bonds, because of their corporate nature and the uncertainties of the business world. There are many factors that can potentially move stocks downward, such as industry competition, internal corporate management, or even mismanagement, and so on. Bonds, on the other hand, are fixed-income products with a relatively secure return (if held to maturity)—except for low-rated, high-return "junk" bonds.

Liquidity risk is primarily associated with bonds since, aside from very small companies, you can pretty much find a buyer for most companies' stock shares whenever you wish. With bonds, however, your money is tied up for a certain period of time. Many people operate under the misperception that bonds are inherently low-risk. While many fixed-income instruments are less risky, some, such as long-term bonds, are quite the opposite. Bond prices are exquisitely sensitive to inflation and interest rates; a big rate hike will make prices take a big drop—an occurrence that will impact a 30-year-bond far more negatively than, say, a short-term-bond.

Now that you know what you're up against, let's see how risk-adverse or risk-tolerant you are.

Test Yourself:
Just How Much Risk Can *You* Tolerate?

As I mentioned earlier, you need to assess your risk tolerance and come to grips with where you stand. You can then use that information to construct a portfolio you can live with on a long-term basis. Take the following quiz, but bear in mind that you'll need to answer the six questions for *each* goal since your responses will most likely vary. Typically, one is willing to accept a greater degree of risk when there is a longer time horizon (say, for a retirement account), as opposed to a liquid account geared toward more immediate goals.

In this quiz (Figure 7.1), be honest. No one will see your responses, so don't concern yourself with what you think the answers *should* be and don't respond the way you *wish* you felt. (If you prefer, you may take the same test online at *www.amerivest.com*; your results will be calculated automatically.)

Risk Tolerance Quiz

Understanding volatility ❓

1. Which concerns you more: day-to-day fluctuations in the value of your investments or the possibility that your investments might not grow enough to meet your long-term goals?

I'm more worried about day-to-day fluctuations.

○ Strongly Agree	○ Agree	○ Neutral	○ Agree	○ Strongly Agree

I'm more concerned about long-term results.

Tolerating losses ❓

2. Imagine that you need to reach your financial goal in 10 years, and you've just invested a portion of your assets specifically toward achieving this goal. In the first year, these assets lose 1/3 of their total value, but evidence suggests that the portfolio should more than double over 10 years - enough to meet your goal. How would you react?

I don't think I could stand it; I'd switch to more conservative investments.

○ Strongly Agree	○ Agree	○ Neutral	○ Agree	○ Strongly Agree

I would still stick with my plan.

Source: www.amerivest.com

Investments that do better in the long run tend to be more volatile over the short run. A more aggressive approach to investing means that you are willing to stick to your investment plan, even during downward trends.

Risk Tolerance Quiz *(continued)*

Sticking to your plan ❷

3. The charts below represent two hypothetical investments. They show the observed value at the end of the first 10 years, as well as the expected value over 20 years. Imagine that Investment 1 is expected to return about 8% per year and Investment 2 is expected to earn about 10% per year. If you faced these two scenarios, which would you prefer?

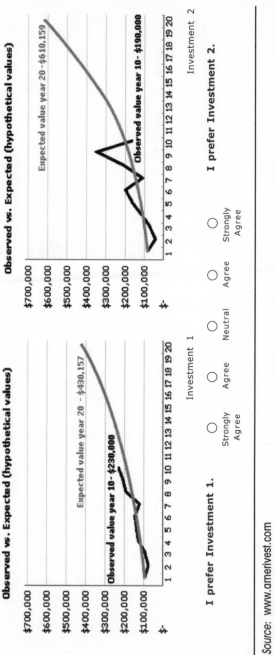

Observed vs. Expected (hypothetical values)

Expected value year 20 - $430,157

Observed value year 10 - $230,000

Investment 1

I prefer Investment 1.

Strongly Agree ○   Agree ○   Neutral ○   Agree ○   Strongly Agree ○

Observed vs. Expected (hypothetical values)

Expected value year 20 - $610,159

Observed value year 10 - $190,000

Investment 2

I prefer Investment 2.

Source: www.amerivest.com

Investments that do better in the long run tend to be more volatile over the short run. A more aggressive approach to investing means that you are willing to stick to your investment plan, even during downward trends.

Accepting the bad with the good ✎

4. Imagine that you're considering five different investments, all of which are expected to at least satisfy your goal. The charts below show the expected range of returns for each of these investments over any single one-year period. The investments with the potential for higher returns also present the possibility of greater risk. Which would you prefer?

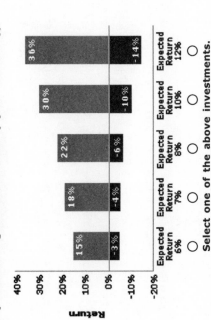

Expected Average Return & Volatility (75% Probability)

Return

Select one of the above investments.

| Expected Return 6% | Expected Return 7% | Expected Return 8% | Expected Return 10% | Expected Return 12% |

Source: www.amerivest.com

Some investors always want to get the most out of their investments, even when less is sufficient to meet their financial goal. This chart illustrates the relationship between risk (standard deviation) and reward (expected return). In general, more aggressive portfolios present a greater volatility of returns. If you'll be satisfied with meeting your goal and aren't attempting to exceed it, your investments should probably be geared toward making slow and steady progress. **Please note:** Actual investments may deviate from expectations due to fluctuations of the market.

Risk Tolerance Quiz *(continued)*

Risk tolerance question 5 of 6: Achieving the right results ❓

5. Choose the statement that best reflects your thoughts about reaching this financial goal:

I'm interested in stable growth in the value of my portfolio, even if it means achieving lower results in the long run.				I'm interested in achieving the maximum growth possible in my portfolio, even if it means accepting significant short-term losses.
○	○	○	○	○
Strongly Agree	Agree	Neutral	Agree	Strongly Agree

Risk tolerance question 6 of 6: Evaluating your experience ❓

6. How much experience do you have investing in the stock and bond markets?

I have little or no experience.				I am very experienced.
○	○	○	○	○
Strongly Agree	Agree	Neutral	Agree	Strongly Agree

Source: www.amerivest.com

Some investors always want to get the most out of their investments, even when less is sufficient to meet their financial goal. In general, more aggressive portfolios present a greater volatility of returns. If you'll be satisfied with meeting your goal and aren't attempting to exceed it, your investments should probably be geared toward making slow and steady progress. **Please note:** Actual investments may deviate from expectations due to fluctuations of the market.

Okay, pencils down. Now evaluate your responses to determine your risk tolerance with the following guidelines:

- Low: If replies are mostly **Strongly Agree** to the left of neutral.
- Low/moderate: If replies are mostly **Agree** to the left of neutral.
- Moderate: If replies are mostly **Neutral**.
- Moderate/high: If replies are mostly **Agree** to the right of neutral.
- High: If replies are mostly **Strongly Agree** to the right of neutral.

Select the appropriate illustration of your risk tolerance (pages 104 and 105). Knowing the degree of risk with which you'll feel comfortable will help you when it comes time to allocating your assets. (We'll get to that in the next chapter.)

No matter whether you can tolerate a "low," "low/moderate," "moderate," "moderate/high," or "high" degree of risk, don't let your rating be your *only* guide. Your age, goals, time frame, personality *and* quiz score are all factors to consider in determining the degree of risk you can accept. For example, if you're a 40-year-old chicken—I mean, ultraconservative investor—and were inclined to put all of your retirement savings into a money fund or cash equivalents, it would be prudent to push the envelope a bit on the risk frontier. Not taking enough risk can sometimes be just as dangerous as taking too much. That said, if the idea of having an account that's 60 percent stocks will keep you up at night or, even worse, give you an ulcer, no amount of return is worth it. The best solution might be to find a middle ground. Likewise, if you have a thrill-seeking personality, you would be wise to rein in your wild side, so you don't risk losing a big chunk of your money—especially if you'll be needing it soon.

Your answers indicate that your risk tolerance is: **Low**

A **Low** risk tolerance means you are an investor who prefers little risk and a lower but steady return. You are likely:

- Comfortable with a low, steady return and taking less risks
- Focused on avoiding the potential for loss
- Not tolerant of fluctuations in the values of your investments

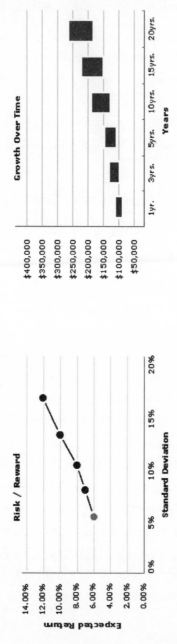

Hypothetical presentation provided for illustrative purposes only. Chart denotes estimated level of risk associated with indicated portfolio expected return. Risk and return can vary based on actual portfolio content.

Source: www.amerivest.com

Using statistical analysis of historical data and long-term projections, we constructed a Capital Preservation portfolio consistent with a low risk tolerance. This portfolio has a 6 percent expected annual total return and 6.96 percent standard deviation.

The chart on the left illustrates the relationship between risk (standard deviation) and reward (expected return). In general, the more aggressive the portfolio is (that is, the higher the expected return), the higher the uncertainty is for achieving that return. It is common to measure this uncertainty with standard deviation. The chart on the right shows how much an initial $100,000 investment in such a portfolio might be worth in 20 years: between $184,180.61 and $255,810.39 (with 75 percent confidence, assuming a normal distribution of returns). **Please note:** Actual investments may deviate from these expectations due to fluctuations of the market. The chart does not reflect the impact of fees, commissions, or taxes. These factors will reduce the expected value of the investment.

Risk Tolerance Quiz *(continued)*

Your answers indicate that your risk tolerance is: **Low / Moderate**

A **Low / Moderate** risk tolerance means you are an investor who prefers a low risk level, but recognizes the necessity for some risk in reaching your goals. You are likely:

- Comfortable with taking a small amount of risk
- Focused on avoiding the potential for loss more than
  the ability for gain
- Tolerant of small fluctuations in the values of your investments

Your answers indicate that your risk tolerance is: **Moderate**

A **Moderate** risk tolerance means you're an investor who prefers to take a modest risk to seek a greater return on your investment. You are likely:

- Comfortable with taking a moderate amount of risk
- Focused equally on the potential for loss and gain
- Tolerant of moderate fluctuations in the values of your investments

Your answers indicate that your risk tolerance is: **Moderate / High**

A **Moderate / High** risk tolerance means you are an investor who takes a substantial amount of risk in order to seek large gains in the value of your investments. You are likely:

- Comfortable with taking a larger amount of risk to achieve greater return
- Focused more on the potential for gain than the idea of loss
- Tolerant of relatively large fluctuations in the value of your investments

Your answers indicate that your risk tolerance is: **High**

A **High** risk tolerance means you are an investor who likes the idea of taking a lot of risk in order to maximize the return on an investment. You are likely:

- Comfortable with taking a large amount of risk to achieve a greater return
- Focused on the ability for your investment to gain in value, and not concerned
  with the potential for loss
- Tolerant of large fluctuations in the value of your investments

Ways to *Contain* Risk

You are not defenseless against risk and can minimize its impact by extending your time horizon, if it's feasible to do so. You may be able to forestall retirement a few years, but you can't ask a college bursar to let you put tuition payments on hold. The longer the time horizon, the more risk is diminished, since an investment has a greater time period within which to recoup losses and rise again. As we've seen, over time, stocks trend upward: Storms calm down, negative returns often turn positive, and bears eventually hibernate (see Table 7.1).

Fixed-income investments are generally considered low-risk, particularly short-term bonds and Treasuries guaranteed by the federal government. You can *almost* avoid credit risk by only going with those that rank highest on two or all three of the top rating agencies: Fitch's Ratings, Moody's, and S&P.

There are many different ways and formulas to measure investment risk. The three most well-known barometers are described below and are easily obtainable on Morningstar.com under mutual fund snapshots' *risk measures*:

TABLE 7.1   Stock Market Risk Diminishes Over Time 1926–2003

	Holding Period (Years)	Annual Return Range	
		Highest Return	Lowest Return
Stocks	1	54%	−43%
Stocks	5	29%	−12%
Stocks	10	20%	−1%
Stocks	15	19%	1%
Stocks	20	18%	3%
Stocks	25	17%	6%

Indices used: Stocks: Large Company Stocks (S&P 500)

Source: Stocks, Bonds, Bills and Inflation® 2004 Yearbook, © 2004 Ibbotson Associates, Inc. Based on copyrighted works by Ibbotson and Sinquefield. All rights reserved. Used with permission.

- *Standard deviation.* This computation reflects how much the security deviates from its average price over a given period of time. The further returns deviate from the mean, the greater the volatility and risk.
- *Beta.* This is a measure of volatility relative to an index (S&P 500 for stocks, Lehman Aggregate Bond for bond funds). It's set at 1.0, so if the beta is higher than 1.0, it's riskier than the market; a stock with a beta of 1.30, for example, is 30 percent more volatile than the stock market. Conversely, if it's lower than 1.0, it's less risky than the market.
- *The Sharpe ratio* measures the risk-adjusted return. As Duncan Richardson puts it, it's "how much you have been paid to take risk."

With an individual equity, the simplest and fastest way to ascertain its level of risk is to check its "business risk" score on Morningstar. You don't have to do the analysis; it's already done for you. The scores are translated into the ratings of *below average, average,* or *above average* and are calculated using the following factors:

- How cyclical is the company's industry?
- How wide is the company's economic moat? (strength of its competitive advantage)
- How strong is the company's balance sheet?
- How does the company's free cash flow compare with its sales?
- How sustainable is the company's operating cash flow?
- How big is the company?
- Is there a nonfinancial issue that could materially affect the company's fortunes?[3]

But far and away, the three *most* important things you can do to temper risk are: diversify, diversify, diversify. Not only do stocks and bonds run in cycles, they tend to run counter to one another—so that when one is driving the ball, the other is more or less sidelined.

Having a healthy mix of assets means you'll almost always be doing well, since either stocks *or* bonds are likely to be advancing.

Creating a mix of different asset classes and different types of investments within those asset classes helps minimize risk. Mary Farrell, author of *Mary Farrell's Beyond the Basics* and UBS's senior investment analyst, concurs: "Diversifying among asset classes helps to even out the risks associated with each type of asset. That is why you might have a portfolio composed of stocks, bonds, and cash equivalents. The particular risk of any asset can be offset to some degree by the specific variability of the other assets in the portfolio."[4]

Diversification goes hand in hand with *asset allocation* (what *weighting* you give to each asset class and subset within each class). If you decide stocks will represent 75 percent of your retirement account, for example, then you further contain risk by breaking down that portion into small-cap, mid-cap, large-cap, international stocks, and so on (see Table 7.2). As Farrell says, "You [allocate assets] to

TABLE 7.2 Risk and Return of Various Asset Classes 1926–2003

	Return	Risk
Small-cap stocks	12.7%	33.3%
Large-cap stocks	10.4%	20.4%
T-Bond	5.4%	9.4%
T-Bill	3.7%	3.1%

Risk is measured by standard deviation, return is represented by compound annual return

Indices used:
Small-cap stocks: Small Company Stocks
Large-cap stocks: Large Company Stocks (S&P 500)
T-Bond: U.S. Long-Term Government Bond
T-Bill: U.S. 30 Day T-Bill

Source: Stocks, Bonds, Bills and Inflation® 2004 Yearbook, © 2004 Ibbotson Associates, Inc. Based on copyrighted works by Ibbotson and Sinquefield. All rights reserved. Used with permission.

minimize risk. For example, if the stock market goes into a correction or bear market, you may benefit from the returns in the fixed-income markets."

Fortunately, the smartest thing you can do to *minimize* risk is also almost universally considered the smartest thing you can do to *maximize* portfolio performance and that brings us to asset allocation.

Coach Moglia's Game Plan

1. *Risk is a part of investing.* Know and accept your risk tolerance. It's an essential factor in putting together a portfolio that you can live with. There's no such thing as a sure thing.

2. There are a number of different types of risk and most pertain to asset classes. *Knowing what they are and how they impact your assets is the key.*

3. *The single best way to contain risk is to diversify your investments.*

chapter eight
ASSET ALLOCATION

It's early in the second quarter and the score is tied at 10 apiece. You're playing a very competitive team, the Tennessee Time-Horizons. They've often outlasted other opponents who didn't quite know how to play against them. Not quick on their feet, they're strong and steady. Your strategy? It's early enough in the game to be able to take some chances and make super-aggressive passes. You've got to be daring to have a shot at getting the ball into the end zone. Sure, the risk of an interception is higher, but it's your best chance to gain a lot of yardage *fast* and build an early lead. Catching up to the Time-Horizons is like rushing uphill.

Another scenario: It's the same team, but now it's late in the fourth quarter and you're winning 24–17. The call? Run the ball. No need to risk anyone getting injured. Play it safe and let the clock run out.

There are many similarities between football strategy and investment strategy. You've got your game clock, or *time horizon.* You also have a certain basic approach: an aggressive offense or a conservative defense; the first is more *risky*, the second is less so.

We've talked about time horizons in the chapter on goals and about risk and its relation to return in the previous chapter. Once you've examined each of these concepts and how they apply to your own life, you're ready to begin constructing your investment portfolio.

The Basics

A portfolio divvied up among stocks, bonds, and cash will *never* perform as well as the highest-performing asset class of the three *at a particular point in time*. So, if you had an all-tech stock portfolio in 1998 and 1999, you would have done unquestionably better than if you had a stock-bond-cash mix. Similarly, if you had an account predominantly composed of three-month Treasury bills in the early 1980s when they were paying 17 percent, you probably trounced the return of most equities. However—notice, there's always a "however"—trying to anticipate *beforehand* which asset class is going to shine, and when its light is about to dim, is a matter best left to psychics and the extremely lucky. There's a funny thing, though, about luck: It runs out. So, to reiterate, unless you are psychic or consistently lucky, you must rely on a stock-bond-cash mix.

In 1986, the results of a landmark study of asset allocation were published in the *Financial Analysts Journal* (and later reconfirmed in 1991). Headed by money manager Gary Brinson, the researchers studied the performance of 92 pension plans. *The study showed that 93.6 percent of portfolio performance could be attributed to asset allocation*. Less than seven percent was linked to specific security selection and market timing.[1] In other words, it didn't much matter *which* stocks or bonds were selected; it was the *diversity*—that there were stocks, bonds, *and* cash—that mattered.

A talented mix is the way to go. Just like team sports. A quarterback, for example, is certainly one of the most key players on a football team, just as a core stock holding is crucial to most portfolios. But if you have a team of *only* quarterbacks, you're in big trouble.

The joint effort of the players in their different positions—how well they work together, how one's strengths compensates for another's weaknesses, how well they protect and balance each other—is what makes a winning team. The same principle applies in investing. The whole is far greater than the sum of its parts and the combination of "players" is what spells success.

Why Stocks, Bonds and Cash Do Mix

The crux of asset allocation is that you capitalize on the fact that different asset classes move in different directions, thereby minimizing risk and reaping the highest possible return. Interest rates, inflation, the leading economic indicators, and other factors affect asset classes differently.

Stocks and bonds have low correlation, meaning they don't move in tandem; when one is doing well, typically, the other isn't. By combining asset classes in a portfolio, you sidestep hazards and reduce the risk of even the most volatile of assets contained within. For example, inflation can be a boon to real estate prices, yet at the same time, it punishes long-term bondholders. Another example is that when U.S. stock markets are in the dumps, international stock markets can be on a tear. Loss in one investment is offset by gains in another.

You're no longer at the mercy of individual security risk or even asset class risk; instead, you deal with—and minimize—risk on an aggregate or larger level. By having your holdings invested in different asset classes, at least one should always be doing well.

Types of Allocation

There are many ways to allocate your investments, but there are three primary types of allocation:

1. *Strategic allocation* takes a passive, long-term view and focuses on buying and holding shifts of stocks, bonds, and cash.
2. *Tactical allocation* is really just market timing in sheep's clothing, in which weightings are adjusted occasionally to capitalize on opportunities that may arise or are anticipated.
3. *Dynamic allocation* allows for frequent shifts in response to changes in the fluid economy and market.

Tactical and dynamic allocations are not wrong, but for the average investor—especially in an account where funds will be needed within the next few years—it's best to stick with strategic allocation. If you're on target for meeting your long-term goals and you want to "play" with a small portion of savings, that's one thing. However, it's best to make a plan and adjust it only at predetermined time intervals.

Where to Begin

The options are almost endless when it comes to choosing which asset classes should be in your portfolio. How much weight each asset class is given depends upon your risk tolerance and time horizon. The asset breakdown of a 40-year-old who is five years away from saving up for a down payment on a vacation condo will be different from that of a 40-year-old who is 25 years away from retirement.

Generally, the further you are from your goal—the longer the time horizon—the more risk you can afford to take and the heavier the recommended weighting in stocks. But *how* heavily weighted? A rule of thumb for the stock portion of a retirement account is to subtract your age from 110. So if you're 45 years old, you should have 65 percent of your 401(k) or IRA assets in equities. A note: When allocating assets, don't forget to look at all your savings as a whole.

If you have \$25,000 in your 401(k) and \$25,000 in a Roth IRA, you could put \$16,250 of *each* account (65 percent of \$25,000) in stocks or have one entire account and just \$7,500 of the other in stocks (a total of 65 percent of \$50,000).

As you approach your goal, you shift the weighting slightly to add more secure, fixed-income investments, like short-term bonds, Treasuries, highly-rated munis, or corporate bonds. Retirees who need to boost monthly income should choose both stocks and bonds that are dividend-driven as well as focused on capital preservation. They should have an eye on growth and capital appreciation as well, since folks are living longer than ever before; a healthy 65-year-old can expect to be around for at least another 15 years.[2]

Table 8.1 and Figure 8.1 represent some model portfolios with straightforward stock-bond-cash components. You'll see that as risk tolerance increases, so does the portion of equities.

TABLE 8.1   Choosing an Asset Allocation

		Average annual return 1926–2003*
80% Stocks/20% Bonds	Growth	9.7%
60% Stocks/40% Bonds	Balanced Growth	8.9%
40% Stocks/ 40% Bonds/20% Cash	Conservative Growth	7.6%
20% Stocks/ 60% Bonds/20% Cash	Income	6.4%

*Average annual return represents a compound annual return.

Indices used:
Stocks: Large Company Stocks (S&P 500)
Bonds: U.S. Long-Term Government Bond
Cash: U.S. 30 Day T-Bill

Source: Stocks, Bonds, Bills and Inflation® 2004 Yearbook, © 2004 Ibbotson Associates, Inc. Based on copyrighted works by Ibbotson and Sinquefield. All rights reserved. Used with permission.

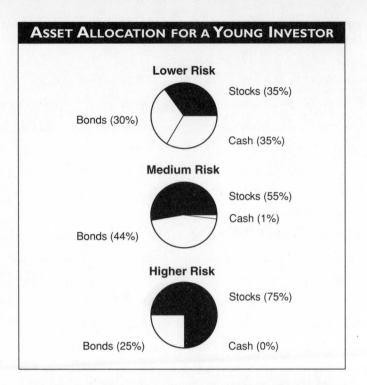

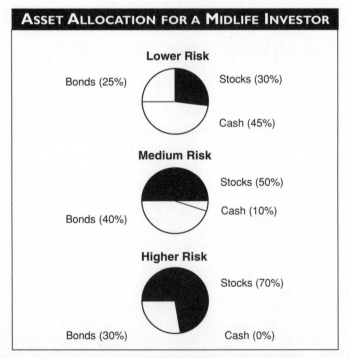

FIGURE 8.1 Model Porfolios for Investors at Different Life Cycles

Source: Ernst & Young's Personal Financial Planning Guide, 3rd ed., John Wiley & Sons, 2000.

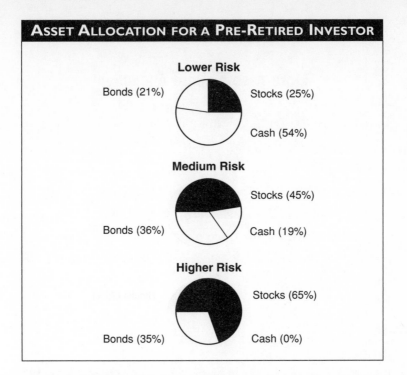

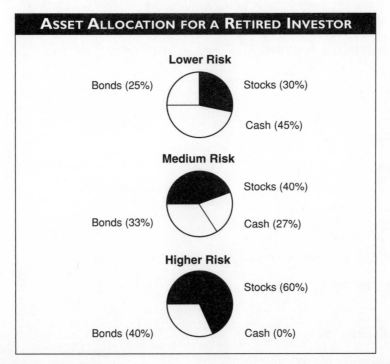

FIGURE 8.1 *(continued)*

More Assets, More Allocation

If you have just a few thousand dollars set aside, it isn't practical to break it up any more than into just the three major asset classes. But if you have, say, $50,000 or more, each asset class should be further allocated among the subcategories of assets. The principle of minimizing risk while maximizing return by diversifying and allocating assets works not just for the three major classes of stocks, bonds and cash; it also works for the subcategories within those classes. Here's a broad overview:

Stocks

Domestic

- Large-cap, mid-cap, and small-cap (subdivisions are growth, value, or a blend of each)

International or **global**

- is further divided into emerging markets, single countries, or single regions

Bonds

Domestic

- Short-term, mid-term, or long-term Treasuries
- Mortgage-backed
- Municipals
- Corporate (highly-rated or lower-rated high-yield)

International

Cash Reserves

- Money markets and short-term CDs

There are other categories as well, such as real estate (including real estate investment trusts, or REITs) and precious metals.

Each subdivision has its owns pros and cons. Small-caps can reap high returns, but they're also very volatile. On the other hand, large-cap stocks tend to be more of a solid, conservative investment than small- or mid-caps. Large-caps are considered the least risky in the same way that a large cruise ship is far safer on the high seas than a kayak. A ship can withstand volatility and not be strewn about the way a small craft would. Therefore, if you were close to retirement, or approaching your goal for a down payment on a second home, you would want to weight large-cap stocks more heavily than small-caps. Similarly, you'd want to have more Treasuries and short-term bond instruments than high-yield junk bonds.

Table 8.2 shows some model portfolios for more substantial or sophisticated portfolios.

TABLE 8.2   Asset Allocation by Category

	Low Risk	
Asset Class		Allocation
Stock	Domestic Large Cap Equities	3%
	Domestic Large Cap Value Equities	5%
	Domestic Mid Cap Equities	2%
	Domestic Small Cap Equities	2%
	Domestic Small Cap Value Equities	2%
	International Developed Equities	10%
	International Emerging Equities	4%
Bond	Real Estate	2%
	Domestic Short Term Government	30%
	Domestic Intermediate Term Government	30%
Cash	Cash	10%

(continued)

TABLE 8.2 *(continued)*

Low/Moderate Risk		
Asset Class		**Allocation**
Stock	Domestic Large Cap Equities	4%
	Domestic Large Cap Value Equities	9%
	Domestic Mid Cap Equities	2%
	Domestic Small Cap Equities	2%
	Domestic Small Cap Value Equities	2%
	International Developed Equities	14%
	International Emerging Equities	4%
Bond	Real Estate	4%
	Domestic Short Term Government	30%
	Domestic Intermediate Term Government	24%
Cash	Cash	5%
Moderate		
Stock	Domestic Large Cap Equities	7%
	Domestic Large Cap Value Equities	14%
	Domestic Small Cap Equities	5%
	International Developed Equities	19%
	International Emerging Equities	5%
Bond	Domestic Short Term Government	19%
	Domestic Intermediate Term Government	30%
Cash	Cash	1%
Moderate/High		
Stock	Domestic Large Cap Equities	11%
	Domestic Large Cap Value Equities	22%
	Domestic Small Cap Equities	5%
	International Developed Equities	23%
	International Emerging Equities	9%
Bond	Domestic Short Term Government	5%
	Domestic Intermediate Term Government	24%
Cash	Cash	1%

TABLE 8.2 *(continued)*

	High	Allocation
Asset Class		
Stock	Domestic Large Cap Equities	15%
	Domestic Large Cap Value Equities	30%
	Domestic Small Cap Equities	5%
	International Developed Equities	27%
	International Emerging Equities	12%
Bond	Domestic Short Term Government	5%
	Domestic Intermediate Term Government	5%
Cash	Cash	1%

Source: Amerivest

So How *Do* You Fill in Your Portfolio's Blanks?

Allocation, shmalocation. When it comes down to it, what should you actually own? I generally don't like to impose my views on others, but since you asked, I think ETFs (exchange-traded funds) are unquestionably the best means to achieving your investment goals. They're cheap and make asset allocation an extremely simple task. ETFs are already set up to track indexes of any and all asset classes or subsets of classes you could possibly want represented—every shade and nuance of stocks and bonds, both domestic and international, as well as real estate, precious metals, and so on.

After the Assets Are Allocated

Even after you have your investments properly allocated and set up in the appropriate accounts, remember that nothing is set in stone. Circumstances change, and accommodations must be made. If you lose your quarterback, you need to replace him with someone else. If a light drizzle becomes a torrential downpour, you may need to switch your strategy from a passing game to a running game to take advantage of a slippery-footed defense. Likewise, work or health challenges or an inheritance windfall would all necessitate a readjustment in how and where savings are invested.

You do *not* want to alter the allocation of your investments as a reaction to blips or dips in the market or economy, but you should adjust your allocation every five years (or more often, once your goal is five years or fewer away) to accommodate your changing time horizon. Keep in mind: Readjusting your allocation is *not* the same as *rebalancing* your portfolio, which we cover in the next chapter.

Coach Moglia's Game Plan

1. If you take away only one bit of information from this book, let it be this: *The mix is more important than the picks.* In other words, successful investing is largely due to asset allocation, not the specific investments you select.
2. The different asset classes don't usually move in lockstep. *When stocks are hot, bonds are often not.*
3. *The guiding principle of investing is to buy and hold for the long term.* The fact that a particular stock, fund, sector, or index is in a slump is not a signal to dump it.
4. *Your risk tolerance and time horizon* are two key factors in determining an appropriate asset allocation.

chapter nine
MONITORING AND REBALANCING

Great portfolios aren't born, they're *made*. And remade and remade and remade.

You see, unlike football, the investing "season" never ends. Sure, it would be nice if you could just craft the perfect portfolio, say "see you in 20 years" and then just walk away—but it isn't quite that simple. As I said in the last chapter, every five years or so, you need to reshuffle the deck, so to speak, to make sure your holdings are still in synch with your time horizon and risk tolerance. The closer you are to needing your money for that vacation home, tuition bill, or retirement, the more you shift into less risky investments, like large-cap, blue-chip stocks or short-term bonds. That's reallocation.

Rebalancing, however, is what you do to make sure your allocation stays put. Let's say, for example, you've apportioned your savings into a 60 percent stock—40 percent bond mix (leaving out cash for the sake of simplicity). The stock market has a bullish year and bonds fall flat. At the end of the year, you look at your portfolio and see it's now 75 percent stocks and 25 percent bonds—quite a different picture. Even though your portfolio has veered way off course from your original allocation, and there's more risk now than you bargained for, it's quite tempting to let that stock portion ride.

The *smart* move, however, is also the most unnatural in the world. In fact, it pretty much flies in the face of human nature. It's as crazy as a football team owner trading the star quarterback for the worst player on another team. Well, almost. The underlying rationale for rebalancing is similar, but with far better results.

Here's how it works: You sell your star performers and buy the underperformers in order to bring your assets back in line with the original allocations you selected. So in the example above, you would sell 15 percent of your equity holdings and buy 15 percent more bonds. It may sound odd at first, but when it comes to your portfolio, it makes perfect sense. You shift the proceeds from superstars to buy more of the laggards because you want to "sell high, buy low." If Wall Street had a motto, that would be it. I hear you thinking, "But if it ain't broke, why fix it?" An investment mix that has strayed from its original allocation is, in a sense, "broke."

What's Wrong with Holding onto Winners

One of the nation's most acclaimed financial advisors, Ric Edelman of Financial Services, Inc. in Fairfax, Virginia, says in his book, *The Truth About Money*:

> If you're buying winners, that means they've already made money, and you thus would be buying after the fact. But selling a winner means you made money with it—and that's the whole point to investing, isn't it? [Y]ou want to buy losers, or more accurately, it doesn't matter if it was a loser before you bought it. All that matters is that it becomes a

winner before you sell it. But if you act emotionally, you'll fail. You'll buy more stocks—"They're making so much money!"—and you'll sell your government securities—"Those dogs! I want to dump them!" In other words, you'll want to buy and sell based on past performance, even though past performance is no indication of future results.[1]

That's why investment decisions should not be based on emotion, greed, or whim. If you let stocks be your everything, for example, that means you've opted to ignore what we already know to be fact: diversification is the key to a winning portfolio.

Let's take that 60 percent stock–40 percent bond mix again, except in this case a grizzly bear market cuts the 60 percent down to 45 percent. By rebalancing and buying more stock when it is cheap, you're positioned to make gains when the market swings back upward. Some asset classes will rise, while others dip; therefore, it's only natural that allocation fluctuates. Your job is to keep all your investments in line. By doing so through rebalancing, you:

- Restore risk to an acceptable level
- Protect gains and take profits off the table
- Buy low, sell high

Know What You *Really* Own

This may seem silly. If you own a stock mutual fund, you own stocks, right? Not necessarily. If the fund manager has the authority and the tendency to move out of equities during times of volatility or uncertainty, that may mean he or she is holding cash on the sidelines, and that also means your allocation may not be what you believe it to be. In truth, your cash holdings are higher and stock holdings are lower. So if you decide to fill your portfolio with a mutual fund, make sure it's one that stays fully invested. That way, if you own a stock fund, you really own stock. If you own a bond fund, you really own bonds.

How would you know whether a manager has the authority and a history of pulling out of the market and staying on the sidelines? If you can't tell from the fund's prospectus, call the fund company and ask a customer service representative how often and how much of the holdings include cash.

Another potential problem that can sabotage allocation as well as rebalancing is duplication. You don't want to own shares of the NASDAQ-100 Index Tracking Stock *and* shares of individual companies that are already represented on that index, for example. Likewise, you wouldn't want to have a health sector ETF and a large growth stock mutual fund that owns a number of pharmaceutical companies already in the index that the ETF tracks. Examine what's in your holdings to avoid duplication or being overly concentrated in one area. A suggestion: Morningstar has a Stock Intersection tool that can electronically crosscheck your holdings for duplication.

The Rebalancing Act: How It's Done

Tax-sheltered accounts—such as 401(k)s, IRAs, and so on—should be realigned by paring down the portion of assets that exceeds its original allotment and using the proceeds to boost the portion of laggards up to its original allotment. Some mutual fund companies and brokerage firms even offer automatic rebalancing features, but trust me, it's easy to do yourself. Simply multiply each percentage—say, 60 percent for stocks—by the total account balance to see precisely how much you should own of that asset. A $50,000 account in that case would require $30,000 in equities. If your equity portion had swelled to $40,000 and your bond portion had deflated to $10,000, you'd sell $10,000 worth of stocks and use the sale proceeds to bulk up the bond piece of the pie.

When it comes to *taxable accounts*, there's more than one way to go. The dilemma is that standouts = profits and realized profits = capital gains. To avoid a hefty capital gains tax bill, rebalance by using *new* money to acquire more of the duds. Another option: You can possibly minimize a hefty tax bill from capital gains by selling the stock shares with the highest cost basis, or purchase price. The higher the cost basis, the lower the capital gains. You can do this with ETFs, individual equities, or mutual funds by selling those shares that cost you the most to buy.

Yet another way to rejigger your holdings in taxable—or even tax-deferred—accounts is to have dividends automatically reinvested, but not in the star investments that generated the income; instead, they're *redirected* into your portfolio's lagging components.

Whichever method you choose to rebalance your portfolio, remember your primary goal: Assets should be readjusted to reflect the level of risk that suits you and the anticipated returns you're seeking. In other words, investments should be rebalanced to be in synch once again with the risk-return formula on which your original allocation was based.

An important note: You can't just realign the major asset classes— stocks, bonds, and cash. It's equally important to have the subsets properly allocated as well. For example, let's say your stock portion equals $40,000 and includes one $20,000 growth investment and one $20,000 value investment (it could be two ETFs, two mutual funds, or two individual equities, or even one of each). The idea is that it's just as important to keep those underlying *types* of equities on target as it is to have equities as a whole on target.

In the year 1999, stocks were trouncing bonds and growth stocks were trouncing value stocks. Your growth stock portion would have grown way out of proportion to what it had been five years earlier. If you had allowed growth stocks to continue to dominate your portfolio by not rebalancing, you would have made yourself extremely vulnerable and suffered the consequences. You would have lost much or all of your gains and missed the opportunity to buy value stocks on the cheap. And when value stocks came back in 2001 and 2002 with a vengeance, the rally would have passed you by.

Asset outperformance goes in cycles. If you cash in your chips on the stock portion that exceeds your original allocation, you may miss out on some further upward movement, but you'll also bypass the drop it will inevitably take—and the losses that go along with it. With a rebalanced portfolio, you keep your profits and use it to beef up the portions that have deflated. Gains that have been made are realized, risk is kept in check, and order is restored.

Resist the temptation to chase past performance and market time; stay the course instead. If you pull out of a lagging sector hoping to catch the current big wave, you'll miss out when that sector turns around. Going in circles means you never get anywhere, so stick to the play—I mean the plan.

When to Rebalance: Pick a Day, Any Day

Although some experts say you should rebalance once your allocations are more than 5 or 10 percent out of whack, the vast majority of experts recommend rebalancing once a year. You don't want to do it more often than once a year, since it may lead to short-term gains—profits on investments held less than a year—and you'll have to pay ordinary income tax, as opposed to just 15 percent on long-term capital gains.

It doesn't really matter which day you pick. How about tax time? Super Bowl morning? Your birthday? Okay, maybe not your birthday, but pick a day, mark it in red on your calendar, and stick to it.

Make sure you don't merely do it within the calendar year; you should have 12 trailing months to be able to get an accurate assessment of performance.

With taxable accounts, there is a plus to *not* rebalancing in the fall, since capital gains are distributed and shareholder dividends are paid out usually sometime from October to the end of December. Rebalancing usually requires purchasing and you don't want to buy a stock or fund just before a distribution is about to be made; otherwise, you'll end up having to pay tax on shares you just bought! So before you leap, look in the prospectus to see when distributions are made; if you can't find the information, ask a representative in the company's shareholder relations or the fund's customer service department.

Tax-Saving Don'ts:

- *Don't* pick investments that are not "rebalance-friendly." Mutual funds with front or back-end loads and redemption fees (if you don't hold them a certain period of time) can be quite punishing. There are more than enough choices out there without these "fines." It's your money. You shouldn't have to be penalized for buying or selling.
- *Don't* pick mutual funds with high turnover. This goes for when you first put together your portfolio, not just for rebalancing. But since you know you're going to be sculpting your holdings—shaving a little here, adding a little there—you might as well pick funds that are tax-conscious so you don't get saddled down with massive capital gains.

Well, you're finally ready to put your plan into action. Where do you begin? With the person you see in the mirror? Another individual? Your computer? A big firm? Let's explore the different options.

Coach Moglia's Game Plan

1. *Investment portfolios are a work in progress.* Even after you craft what you think is an ideal mix, you must periodically revisit to tweak and adjust the proportions as well as the components. There's Christmas Day. There's Mother's Day. Be sure to "celebrate" Rebalancing Day once a year.

2. *Rebalancing can be emotionally challenging,* since it requires you to sell investments that have made you money and to buy more of what lost you money. Get over it.

3. With taxable accounts, limit investment sales that will trigger taxable gains. *Rebalance with **new** money to acquire more of the underperformers.*

chapter ten
EXECUTE YOUR INVESTMENT PLAN

In Part One, we learned the rules of the game. In Part Two, we have talked about strategy. We've done the blackboard training, so you know the Xs and Os of investing. You have the knowledge and the ability; you are equipped and conditioned. Here we go: It's almost time for the coin toss.

Investing is not brain surgery, although Wall Street does all it can to get you to believe it's very technical and complicated. They have a vested interest in doing so, as you can see from Robert T. Kiyosaki's *Rich Dad's Guide to Investing*:

> *The world of investing looks like a professional football game. You have the TV commentators describing the play-by-play battle of the blue chip giants on the field. There are the adoring fans purchasing shares instead of tickets, cheering for their favorite team…there are the bookmakers, called stockbrokers, who give you stock quotes over the phone and record your bets. What most people do not see in both arenas of the sports world and the investment world is what is going on behind the scenes. And that is the **business** [emphasis added] behind both games….*

It's the business behind the business that makes money regard-
less of who wins the game or which way the market goes—up or
down. It's the business that sells *the tickets to the game; it does*
not buy the tickets.[1]

There you have it. The fact is that financial firms make their
money from selling tickets, or investments, to you. They make their
money whether you make money or not. Those on Wall Street don't
want those on Main Street to think they can invest on their own
because the "pros" only make money if you feel you *need* them, in
which case you'll *pay* them. However, we've already talked about
how market timing and stock-picking success is unreliable at best. In
fact, a recent study proved that market timers actually lose money
instead of making healthy profits.[2] It's highly unlikely that this year's
winning stock or fund will cop top prize next year. The *only* way to
consistently win on a long-term basis is to diversify, allocate your
assets, and then simply stay invested.

The very first thing you need to do before you can begin executing your plan is to open a brokerage account. You can't play ball
without a field. A brokerage account allows you to purchase securities and gives you the backdrop against which to implement your
plays. There are a number of different choices when it comes to brokerage firms. I firmly believe that flying solo is the way to go—and
you have all you need to be airborne.

The Self-Directed Investor:
You and an On-Line Brokerage Firm

As I've said before—and will say again—I believe that you can
create your own portfolio. Even if you get some help on that front,
however, it isn't necessary to have someone else put your plan into

action, by making the appropriate purchases and sales. I believe that trading on-line can be as simple as pie and dirt cheap. Of course, it wasn't always an option. It used to be that you had to go to a full-service brokerage firm and pay through the nose to buy a stock. All that changed 30 years ago, when brokers' commissions were deregulated and the discount brokerage industry was born.

Today, there are about 10 or so major on-line discount brokers. The least expensive way to execute a trade is to do so online. You can make a trade for less than $11 at an on-line deep discount broker, but that same trade will cost you $100, give or take, at a full-service brokerage firm.

If you're wondering just how on-line brokers can operate for so much less, it's because they simply don't have the enormous overhead (offices, staff, etc.) of full-service firms. The distinction exists even among discount on-line brokers. If you do a little comparison shopping, you'll see that, in general, the greater the overhead—the more walk-in branch offices, for example—the higher the cost of a trade. Read the fine print. Sometimes, you'll see trades advertised for a super-low price, but when you look closely, it requires a minimum number of trades in order to qualify for that low rate.

On-line brokers give you 24-hour access to your account, investment research, and educational tools, as well as real-time tech support, price quotes, and price alerts. Even if you have an account with an on-line broker, you can still opt to make trades electronically via phone or by what's called broker-assisted trades. The fee will be higher, however, than if you simply do it yourself online.

A caveat: It's essential for any professional you deal with to be objective. And this holds true with advisors or brokers you may come into contact with through an on-line brokerage firm. When you buy shares from one of, say, Charles Schwab's or E*Trade's proprietary mutual funds that bear the company's name, you should know that the brokerage will directly profit from the fees you pay. This doesn't mean the funds are "bad." It's simply that advice or research and sales should not overlap.

On a practical and important note, remember that whether you're a do-it-yourselfer or an advisor's client, *always* make sure you receive transaction statements to double check trades were executed correctly, and to keep updated records.

If you still feel uneasy about going it alone and want a little hand-holding, that's okay. Some people start out that way and *then* go off on their own. Either way, it's important to understand your alternatives: what each provides and what it doesn't.

Financial Planners

There's an entire alphabet soup of professional designations out there. Don't be so impressed by letters until you know what they mean. CPA-PFS is a certified public accountant with additional personal finance training. ChFC stands for Chartered Financial Consultant and signifies an insurance expert with investment training (see Table 10.1) The different types of "experts" are numerous and who's best varies depending upon your needs, but let's confine ourselves to the roads *most* traveled.

A financial advisor can help you assess your risk tolerance, diversify and allocate your assets, and channel savings into the appropriate accounts. It's very important to keep in mind, however, that anyone with a hammer and some nails can hang out a shingle and call himself/herself a financial planner. Don't assume that means he or she possesses any particular investment expertise or training. Also, depending upon whether the individual planner has a license to trade securities, you may have to be the one to implement the advice on your own.

TABLE 10.1 Categories of Financial Professionals

	NAPFA: National Association of Personal Financial Advisors	CFP: Certified Financial Planner	AICPA/PFS: Certified Public Accountant with Personal Financial Specialist	ChFC: Chartered Financial Consultant
Compensation	Fee-Only all of the time	Fees and/or commissions	Fees and/or commissions (with disclosure)	Fees and/or commissions
Continuing Education Required	60 hours every two years. Includes at least five hours in each of six areas of financial planning. Each hour documented and records subject to audit.	30 hours every two years. Includes at least two hours in ethics. Each hour documented and records subject to audit.	60 points in personal financial planning, business experience and life-long learning every three years.	30 hours every two years.
Peer Review Requirements	Peer review of a sample comprehensive financial plan is a requirement of membership.	None stated.	Submit references, if requested, to substantiate financial business planning business experience.	None stated.

(continued)

TABLE 10.1 *(continued)*

	NAPFA: National Association of Personal Financial Advisors	CFP: Certified Financial Planner	AICPA/PFS: Certified Public Accountant with Personal Financial Specialist	ChFC: Chartered Financial Consultant
Experience Required for Admission	Minimum 36 months engaged primarily in the provision of comprehensive financial planning services within the last 60 months, and including the most recent 12 months.	With a bachelor's degree, three years working in the financial planning field. If no bachelor's degree, then five years working in the financial planning field.	Minimum of 25 points in PFP experience within the five-year period preceding application.	Three years business experience. A bachelor's or graduate degree may qualify for one year.
Education Required for Admission	Three credits of advanced education in each of the following: income taxes, investments, estate planning, retirement planning and risk management.	10-hour, two-day comprehensive exam covering more than 100 financial planning topics.	CPA with at least 100 points earned under the multiple entry point system, which includes passing a financial planning exam.	Complete eight financial planning courses.

Source: NAPFA

When a financial planner is *certified* (CFP), it indicates that she has a certain degree of experience, has passed a 10-hour exam and has agreed to comply with a code of ethical conduct laid out by CFP Board of Standards, called the Code of Ethics of Professional Responsibility. Generally, CFPs are compensated with a combination of both a set fee (from the client) as well as commissions (from the companies whose products they sell). The ethical code to which they must adhere requires that they act only in a client's best interests and not make a recommendation that's contingent on the sale of a financial product.

Fee-Only Financial Advisors

A Registered Investment Advisor (RIA or simply IA), also sometimes referred to as a Registered Financial Advisor, is a financial planner licensed by the National Association of Personal Financial Advisers. IAs are considered a fiduciary of their clients and work in a "fee-only" arrangement. That means they are purely compensated by you, the client, and that they do not receive commissions or fees for selling or recommending that you invest your money in any particular product. Their compensation comes from a set fee that you pay—no matter which assets, investments, or brand names you select. Payment can be based on a project fee, a retainer fee, or an hourly fee (it ranges but can be anywhere from $200 to $400 per hour). It can also be structured as a percentage of assets under management (AUM); one percent is typical, but it can run from as little as .50 percent to as high as 1.5 percent. The greater your assets, the smaller the fee.[3]

They must meet stringent requirements in different areas, such as education; becoming a CFP is one way an IA can satisfy the educational portion of his or her requirements. IAs offer comprehensive portfolio analysis. If you ask for help with one portion of your savings—say, just your 401(k)—they'll want to examine your entire financial situation. It's analogous to being a good doctor. If you go in complaining of stomach pain, they won't just give you a pill to make the pain go away. They'll do a complete physical and take tests to get a whole and accurate assessment of your health.

An IA who manages $25 million or more is required to register with the Securities Exchange Commission (SEC) and file an "ADV form."[4] About 75 percent of IAs manage less than $25 million, so they can register with the state securities agency instead of the SEC. Interview two or three prospective candidates to see if you feel comfortable with him or her and to review his or her credentials. Ask for and examine the ADV form that will tell you about an advisor's designation and experience. Part One will tell you if there have been any disciplinary actions taken against the advisor, as well as the number of clients he or she retains, and so on. Part Two indicates fees and services. You can obtain information pertaining to an IA's registration either from the SEC or from the applicable state agency; locate yours from the North American Securities Administrators Association (see Resources).

IAs may require investors to have a minimum balance to open an account. If you don't meet the minimum but they're smart, they may still give you some general guidance as a jump-start. That way, if you need counsel down the road once your assets grow enough to meet the minimum, you may become a client. Get a referral to advisors in your area on the National Association of Personal Financial Advisor's Web site, or call 800.366.2732.

The Full-Service Brokerage Firm

The large brokerage firms—also called wirehouses—employ stockbrokers who are licensed by the National Association of Security

Dealers to sell securities. Brokers earn commissions from the trades you make, as well as on many of the investments you buy (sometimes an account is "wrapped," in which case you pay a flat fee based on the amount of assets under management).

A stockbroker at a full-service brokerage firm:

- Has access to research performed by departments staffed with analysts, all trying to assess the future potential of thousands of securities
- Will advise you on which investments to buy and sell—and when
- Has trades executed on your behalf

Sounds ideal, right? Well, there's one problem—and it's a big one. The top qualities a client should look for in a financial advisor are objectivity and trust. If you cannot be *assured* that the advice given is in your best interests, you're headed down the wrong path. You would be likely to pay thousands of dollars unnecessarily over the years.

Many large brokerage firms are also investment banks that underwrite issues of stocks and bonds and then sell those products to their clients. It's like a grocery store featuring the store's own brand up front and tucking other equal but cheaper brands in the back on a bottom shelf.

In addition, some mutual fund companies pay commissions to brokerage firms—which they may, in turn, share with their brokers—for selling their funds. These are the "load" funds in which part of the load represents the broker's commission and the firm pays it up front. A firm can cover itself by charging a back-end redemption fee that diminishes as time goes on. If you buy a fund with a five percent back-end load, the percentage will drop down gradually each year. Once you've been in the fund a certain number of years and the firm has, in a sense, been reimbursed—by you!—for compensating the broker, the load is eliminated. With bonds, you pay commission—also called "the spread"—based on the difference between what the brokerage paid and what it charges you. In addition, brokers are generously compensated for selling you—and *keeping* you—in certain fee-laden products like annuities.

As you can see, the problem is that the stockbroker works for a *firm*. His or her allegiance is to the firm. And while a brokerage firm cannot legally compensate a broker *specifically* for selling the company's own products, the fact is that a stockbroker will earn commissions, and perhaps bonuses, by doing so. A broker may, therefore, be motivated to boost his or her income by selling you shares of the company's own Frank's Full-Service Mutual Fund or an annuity, even though it's riddled with loads and other fees, and there are other equally lucrative, less costly choices available.

This is not to say that stockbrokers don't want you to make money or are not to be trusted. It's simply that you should be confident that the advice you receive is not tainted in any way. The advisor should not benefit financially from your investment decisions. Even the appearance of impropriety should be avoided. And when someone is profiting by promoting pricey Product A instead of Product B with paltry fees, can you be *sure* that his or her advice is completely objective? Can you be sure that he or she has your—*and only your*—best interests at heart? Stockbrokers are human and may be swayed when they're going to benefit financially from the advice they give. So if you're going to need an advisor, it should be someone who has nothing to gain by the specific products he or she recommends.

Another downside to the traditional brokerage houses is *trading costs*. While the cost varies depending upon your AUM, at say, a typical $100 bucks a pop, you're talking hundreds or thousands of dollars, depending upon how many trades you make. It can add up quickly. So can account management fees.

According to the groundbreaking book *Data Driven Investing*, by Bill Matson and Mitch Hardy, the financial services industry is stacked against the small investor. They describe the conflicts of interests that pollute analysts' recommendations and criticize the high fees charged by the majority of mutual fund and full-service brokerage firms.[5] A recent survey showed that even the wealthy have caught on.[6] High–net worth individuals are choosing to go it alone rather than enlisting the aid of financial advisors. A prominent reason? Fees. They simply didn't feel the service they received justified the fees they had to pay.

Finally, when you receive advice from a financial professional, be aware of the possible existence of industry bias. For example, a stockbroker will lean toward packing your portfolio with equities, a bond broker will have a bond bias, and an insurance expert will likely favor annuities. It's human nature. People recommend what they know best.

Should you decide to consider a full-service broker—whether it's because Aunt Tilly swore by Frank's Financial Services or for some other reason—be *sure* to ask a stockbroker these questions before making investment decisions:

- Why do you think this stock/bond/annuity is right for me? How does it fit in with my investment goals and risk tolerance?
- What is your commission on this stock/bond/annuity? Are you being given any other special incentives to sell this recommendation? [You have a right to know any and all ways in which products you purchase or invest in may benefit a broker.]
- Does your firm or any subsidiary of your firm manage this fund or product?
- If it is a stock: Are you buying this stock out of your firm's inventory? If your firm is rating this stock a buy, why is your firm selling the stock from its inventory?
- Did your company underwrite the stock?

- Why are you recommending this purchase now as opposed to some other time?
- Will you show me your account so I can see that you own what you are selling to me? On any product or service, ask the brokers to print their personal accounts from the computer and show you what they own and especially if they own what they're selling to you. [Yes, this is a legitimate request. If a broker raves about a particular stock but hasn't purchased any for himself or herself, it's reasonable to ask why not.]
- What is the standard deviation of this investment and how does this affect the standard deviation of my portfolio? (Reminder: Standard deviation is a measurement of volatility and risk. See Chapter 7.)[7]

As we've seen, there are many different avenues for investment guidance. However, I firmly believe that you can do it yourself. Simply take the risk tolerance quiz, determine an appropriate asset allocation and break it down along the lines of what was presented in Chapter 8. Open an investment account at a quality on-line broker where trades are simple and cheap. Then just plug in the respective gaps for each asset or subasset class; for example, an S&P 500 exchange-traded fund or index fund can represent the large-cap portion. Set it on "automatic," stopping only to rebalance yearly and to tweak your asset allocation as time goes by.

In the final analysis, you're the commentator, the quarterback, the coach, and the owner of the team, all rolled into one. So get in the game, stay on top of it, and you'll come out a winner. Now take the ball and run with it.

Coach Moglia's Game Plan

1. Y*ou have all that's necessary to handle your own investments.*
2. *Don't give your money away unnecessarily.* Create and re-create your portfolio using a well-known and cost-effective on-line brokerage service.
3. If you feel you need a little handholding, *go with a fee-only registered investment advisor* who has no profit motivation that could possibly bias his or her recommendations.
4. *But **don't** relinquish **total** control to any one else.* Even if you hire an advisor, insist on quarterly reviews and stay involved. This can eliminate surprises; small problems have a way of getting bigger if they aren't addressed regularly!

PART THREE
The Postgame Show

chapter eleven

A NEW WAY TO INVEST

O kay. We've spent the last 10 chapters coaching you on the fundamentals of investing—showing you how to use your financial assets like a good football coach runs his team. By now, you should have a pretty good idea about when to be aggressive and when to play it safe.

Now I'm going to take a little more time explaining what Wall Street used to be like, how it changed and how Ameritrade is giving momentum to self-directed investors like you.

Thirty years ago, the investment world was like an exclusive country club in which wealthy Americans paid high dues (in the form of commissions) to have skilled brokers select stocks and bonds and execute trades on their behalf. While these affluent clients played ball with their full-service broker-dealers, the majority of America sat it out on the sidelines. The middle class melting pot—the real heart of America—was relegated to traditional bank savings accounts. There was little in the way of financial literacy and the elitist investment banks had no motivation to include those that couldn't afford to pay fat commissions.

Fast forward to 2002. Half of all Americans households share in the investment opportunities once limited to the upper crust. About 84.3 million Americans own stock. More the 93 million shareholders hold stakes in U.S. mutual funds. By October 2004, those 93 million investors had shares worth $7.651 trillion! What sparked this enormous sea change?

On May 1, 1975—remembered as "May Day"—the SEC pulled the plug on clubby price fixing. Its groundbreaking ruling deregulated commissions meaning that they would now be set by market forces. Brokerage firms would now have to face some upstarts who dared to chip away at the old-school exorbitant fee structure, letting the "little guys" in on the action at affordable prices. A trade that would once have cost hundreds—even thousands of dollars in 1970—would soon cost less than $100—and, quite soon, much less than that.

Companies soon sprang up to give traders and investors a much better deal—a deal that would one day be more than 20 times better! One of those new kids on the block was Ameritrade. Its founders and my predecessor, J. Joe Ricketts, had a vision for the brave new world of deregulation and founded one of America's first discount brokers.

Ameritrade and firms like it grew by leaps and bounds. By 1997, when Ameritrade went public, we had helped change the face of investing forever. Technology has advanced rapidly and now self-directed investors can trade and manage their portfolios on-line with confidence, speed, and minimal expense. Whether in the comfort of their own homes or halfway around the world, clients have the power to place trades at any time of day or night, with a few clicks of a computer mouse.

The Ameritrade model has attracted millions of clients and thousands more are joining us every week. Our clients and the nearly 100 million other American investors are dividing the pie of total American wealth into innumerably more slices than ever before.

Ordinary American families are saving for college, building for retirement, starting businesses, buying second homes, traveling worldwide and growing their assets; it is all supported in large part by intelligent, disciplined investing.

Today, owning a stock portfolio is really as commonplace as shopping at Wal-Mart. All the tools—streaming quotes, charts, detailed histories of price trends and volumes by stocks, stop and limit orders, and more—are literally at the fingertips of anyone with a computer and the desire to better himself or herself financially. Most orders are executed and confirmed in seconds. Like cell phones and satellite TV, on-line trading is truly an everyday, underappreciated, accessible, and valuable tool.

But at one of the world's largest on-line brokerage firms, Ameritrade knows that trading is just one investing need of the individual.

Investing for the long term is another need that many of our clients tell us is not well served by mutual fund companies or full service brokerages. With our low-cost trading platform and automated tools, we can provide an investing program that is well suited to the needs of long-term investors.

Estimates of this group are all over the place, but it generally appears that 37 million households in the United States have between $100,000 and $1,000,000 in investable assets. That's an aggregate market of more than $11 trillion. The problem is that many in this group don't have enough individual assets to get attention from professional advisors and money managers. But their need for help is very real and, frankly, is the lifeblood of our economy.

Ameritrade Holding will announce a number of new services aimed at this large and fast-growing group—but we've already launched one that we think may do nothing less than change the face of investing. Again.

We call it Amerivest.® It's an online investment advisory service we offer through Amerivest Investment Management, LLC, a subsidiary registered investment adviser. We're pretty excited about Amerivest because it makes intelligent, diversified, logically allocated investing more simple and affordable for the average investor. Frankly, we think there's nothing else quite like it. The biggest problem we've had in telling the world about Amerivest is that it just seems too good to be true.

So let me ask you. How would you like an investing process that—

- Spreads your risk over hundreds of stocks and bonds?
- Provides both domestic and international exposure?
- Is designed to produce returns based on your individual goal and risk tolerance, utilizing products created to track specific market indexes.
- Costs you a fraction of what other investments might charge you, both up-front, and year after year?
- Takes you about an hour or less on your computer, both for initial setup and periodic rebalancing?

What did I tell you? It does sound too good to be true. But believe me, its real and it is working today. Lower fees means more of your investable assets stay invested! Keep reading—you'll be amazed.

We have created an online investment advisory service that levels the Wall Street playing field for long-term investors the same way our brokerage model levels it for active traders.

Enter Amerivest.

Amerivest combines technology, innovation, revolutionary low pricing, and a commitment to help small investors beat the financial game that's often rigged against them—by simply going around it.

The process starts with exchange-traded funds (ETFs), an ingenious (10 years old) investment pioneered by the American Stock Exchange. ETFs now represent more than $160 billion in assets, with some of the biggest-volume individual securities.

As I said in Chapter 5, each share of an ETF buys you a basket of securities. A single share of the SPDR ETF buys you a piece of all 500 stocks in the S&P 500. The risk of your $120 investment is instantly spread across 500 stocks. Thereafter, your investment closely tracks the performance of the S&P 500 "basket" of 500 securities. You buy an entire portfolio with one click!

The same goes for QQQQ, which buys you a basket of the top 100 NASDAQ tech stocks. And the Russell 3000, which buys you 3000 securities in one swipe! The SPDR is one of the biggest dollar-volume security in today's financial landscape. The QQQQ is the most heavily traded.

ETFs are ideal—they give you lots of choice and plenty of diversity—at *very* low cost. But which ETFs are right for you? Using ETFs and other related investments, Amerivest employs our proprietary technology to calculate a portfolio based on your risk tolerance, goal, and time frame.

How do we know what portfolio fits your long-term needs and stomach for risk? We ask you! We take you through a few simple questions. You tell us how much risk you're willing to take. You tell us how much you have to invest now—and expect to have each month going forward. You tell us how much money you're going to need in the future—say, for college tuition in 15 years, or for retirement in 20 years.

With our asset allocation models, we put together a portfolio of ETFs tailored to your goals and your profile—be it conservative, aggressive, or in-between.

In a second or two, we serve up our recommendations. At this point, if you are comfortable with our advice, you open an Ameritrade Investing Account online. The recommended trades are carried over, and you can purchase the entire portfolio through Ameritrade with one click of the mouse. Quickly and efficiently, your money is diversified in hundreds of stocks and bonds across the broad market—at the risk level you're comfortable with.

And here's the most amazing part—by investing in indexed products like ETFs, on average you're very likely to outperform most actively managed mutual funds. The track record for indexed investments like ETFs is very, very good. Only a small percentage of non-indexed funds have posted better returns—and this year's hot fund may be next year's also ran.

So Amerivest is fast, fun, the process is easy, the portfolio is designed around your individual goals and risk tolerance—and what else? Oh, yeah—price.

For accounts between $20,000 and $100,000, Amerivest will cost you just 50 basis points a year—that's the financial world's fancy way of saying ½ percent. If you invest more that $100,000, you get a 30 percent discount and the fee is only 35 basis points. That's just about ⅓ of one percent! For accounts less than $20,000, the fee is variable, but never more than $25 per quarter. Many mutual funds charge you up to 5.75 percent sales charge to get in. With Amerivest, there are no Ameritrade brokerage commissions. Even no-load mutual funds typically have a larger annual expense ratio than ETFs. The average annual total costs for actively managed mutual funds could be three times your Amerivest "50 basis points." Add in an advisor's fee and you are talking big money—big money you could be losing by investing in conventional mutual funds. Why? Because those sales charges, fees, and higher annual expenses cut directly into your return, possibly costing you tens of thousands—even hundreds of thousands of dollars over 15, 20, or 30 years.

Yet despite the cost and performance advantages of Amerivest, the initial investment process literally will take you about half an hour. It all seems way too easy—to put together a personalized, diversified, properly allocated long-term portfolio in less time that it takes to watch a TV rerun!

There is one final step—rebalancing. The portfolio we create for you today may be great, but as the stock and bond market changes— as some companies flourish and others struggle—your baskets of securities will gradually drift out of balance, out of whack with the goals and risk tolerance you established up front. So every few months—and at least once a year—you should get into your account, indicate that you want to rebalance your Amerivest portfolio—and then you should execute the recommendation Amerivest generates for you.

Some of your ETFs will be sold, and others purchased, to bring you back to the ideal portfolio for the long-term needs of you and your family.

The creation of Amerivest is one of my proudest achievements as Ameritrade's CEO, and it is the end result of work by hundreds of people on our dedicated team.

Amerivest is cheaper, faster and more fun than many other ways to invest for the long-term—I told you it sounds too good to be true. To learn more, and to put together your own Amerivest portfolio, go to *www.amerivest.com*. You'll enjoy the process—even if you don't decide to invest now—because it's all built around *your* needs, desires, goals, and attitudes.

Amerivest is just one of many new products and services we're inventing for the mass affluent market. Ameritrade's aim is to be *the* on-line trading platform both for active traders and long-term investors—for both your short-term trading dollars *and* your long-term investment dollars.

Well, it's late in the fourth quarter, and time for you and me to finish the game. Any coach's game plan or playbook doesn't mean much until it's played out on the gridiron. The same with the investment fundamentals I've outlined for you here.

It's time to take charge of your financial life. Believe me, no one else will. Put together a plan and start reaching for those financial goals. Talk to an advisor if you like, but remember—only you care passionately about your money and what you can do with it.

My final coach's command is this: Don't put it off! Millions of Americans just let their finances and investments drift along, with no real plan or understanding. That's the surest way to lose in the market—by doing nothing. The dollars you worked so hard to earn—those precious extra dollars you struggled to set aside for the future—will just drift away, day by day, until you wind up with only a fraction of what you deserve.

Take charge! You can do it. Review my coach's tips at the end of each chapter. Start repositioning your assets so they make real sense—and so you and your family have a better chance to get everything in the future you've dreamed of and sweated so hard for.

Financial success is in *your* hands—and no one else's. Start your game plan today!

GLOSSARY

12b-1 fee: A mutual fund expense levied to help reimburse a fund's sponsor for distribution costs and commissions.

401(k) plan: A retirement plan offered by a corporation to its employees, which allows employees to set aside income into an account. Contributions and earned income are tax-deferred until withdrawn for retirement purposes. The name 401(k) comes from the IRS section describing the program.

529 plans: Named for Section 529 of the Internal Revenue Code, these are vehicles to help parents save and pay for college. One type is called a college savings plan, in which parents can deposit money into an account for their child's college expenses. They can select from any state's plan. Assets grow tax-deferred and earnings are exempt from federal, and sometimes state, taxes. The other type is called a prepaid tuition plan, in which parents pay for college years in advance at a locked-in tuition rate, thereby avoiding steep tuition hikes and sometimes cutting costs by as much as half.

Accreted interest: The difference between par value of a zero-coupon security and purchase price. Also called original issue discount. Yearly accreted interest is the amount of accreted interest "earned" each year that you hold a zero-coupon investment.

Accrued interest: Interest earned but not yet paid. The amount of interest that the buyer owes the seller on transactions involving fixed-income securities, such as most bonds and notes.

Adjustment bonds: Bonds issued in exchange for outstanding bonds when recapitalizing a corporation that faces bankruptcy.

Aggressive growth funds: Mutual funds that focus on small-company stocks that have the potential for accelerated earnings.

Allocation: The process of deciding which investment (choice or combination of choices) best fits your goals, time horizons, and capital availability.

Alpha: A measure of selection risk (also known as residual risk) of a mutual fund in relation to the market. A positive alpha is the extra return awarded to the investor for taking a risk, instead of accepting the market returns. For example, an alpha of 0.4 means the fund outperformed the market-based return estimate by 0.4 percent. An alpha of −0.6 means a fund's monthly return was 0.6 percent less than would have been predicted from the change in the market alone.

Alternative minimum tax: Federal income tax intended to make sure that almost all individuals—especially the wealthy—pay some tax.

American Stock Exchange (AMEX): A major stocks and options exchange located at 86 Trinity Place, New York, New York.

Analyst: An employee of a brokerage firm or mutual fund who studies companies and makes buy and sell recommendations on their stocks. Most specialize in a specific industry.

Annual percentage rate (APR): The total cost of a loan per year, including both interest charges and most or all fees.

Annual percentage yield (APY): The total income an investment earns per year. The APY generally represents the total earnings of a cash account such as a money market fund or savings account, though it forms only part of the returns from stocks and bonds, which can also experience capital growth.

Annual report: An audited report of a corporation's year-end financial results and operations, filed annually with the SEC. The report contains detailed information related to the company's financial condition, legal liabilities, and plans for the upcoming year. Shareholders may obtain a free copy of this report from the corporation.

Annual report (mutual fund): A report that gives an overview of a fund's performance and operations.

Annuity: A contract usually with an insurance company in which the individual makes either a lump-sum payment or periodic payments to the insurance company and in return receives the repayment of principal and earnings as income for a specified number of years or a lifetime.

Ask (asked price): The lowest price a security is offered for sale.

Asset: Any holding that has monetary value, such as a house, a car, or jewelry. Financial assets include stocks, bonds, and real estate.

Asset allocation: The percentage breakdown of how assets are invested in a portfolio. The primary asset categories of a portfolio are cash, bonds, and stocks.

Automatic investment plan: A plan in which a fixed sum is regularly deducted from your paycheck or bank account, then automatically invested in a mutual fund, 401(k) plan, or retirement investment account.

Average: Also known as an index, a mathematical computation that indicates the value of a number of securities as a group. The three most popular averages are the Dow Jones Industrial Average (DJIA), Standard & Poor's (S&P) 500, and the New York Stock Exchange Composite. The average—which may be market-weighted, share-weighted, or price-weighted—indicates performance.

Back-end load: A special charge assessed when mutual fund shares are redeemed. These charges often decrease over time.

Balance sheet: An accounting statement reflecting the firm's financial condition in terms of assets, liabilities, and net worth (ownership). In a balance sheet, Net Worth = Assets + Liabilities.

Bear market: A market in which prices of securities are generally declining.

Beta (mutual funds): The measure of a mutual fund's rate of return in relation to the market. A beta of 0.7 means the fund's total return is likely to move up or down 70 percent of the market change; a beta of 1.3 means total return is likely to move up or down 30 percent more than the market.

Beta (stocks): The measure of a stock's volatility in relation to the market. A beta of 0.7 means a stock price is likely to move up or down 70 percent of the market change; a beta of 1.3 means the stock is likely to move up or down 30 percent more than the market.

Bid: The highest price anyone has declared that he or she is willing to pay for a security.

Blend funds: Also called a hybrid fund, this is a mutual fund with stocks, bonds, and cash, instead of just one or two of those assets. It gives investors asset diversification in a single fund. The mix usually stays fixed, unlike an asset allocation fund where there are the three main asset classes, but the manager can generally divvy it up as he or she sees fit to maximize performance.

Blue-chip: A term used to describe the common stocks of corporations with the strongest of reputations for generating earnings and paying dividends.

Bond: 1. A debt instrument; a security that represents the debt of a corporation, a municipality of the federal government, or any other entity. A bond is usually long-term in nature (10 to 30 years) and is to be repaid to investors on a specified date.

2. An investment in a government or corporation that is structured very much like a loan, only the payment is to individual bondholders rather than to a lending institution. Most bonds offer a regular, scheduled income, making them attractive to retirees and others living off their investments.

Bond fund: A type of mutual fund that invests in bond and preferred stocks with the idea of providing a stable income with a minimum of risk.

Breaking the buck: Refers to a money market fund dipping below its net asset value of $1.00 per share.

Broker: 1. An individual who buys or sells securities for clients (a stockbroker).

2. On an exchange, one who executes public orders on an agency basis (a floor broker or commission house broker).

3. As a slang term, a firm that executes orders for others (a brokerage firm).

Brokerage firm: A partnership or corporation that is in business to provide security services for its clients.

Bull market: A market in which prices of securities are generally rising.

Callability: The feature of a bond whereby the corporation that has issued it can redeem the bond before it matures. Corporations may call their bonds when interest rates drop below their current bond rates. They may then replace high-yielding bonds with lower-yielding bonds.

Callable bonds: Bonds that can be redeemed by the issuer before maturity.

Capital: 1. The total amount of money invested in a firm.

2. Money accumulated and available to be used to produce more money.

Capital gain: A profit resulting from the sale of tangible property. Capital assets which are owned for one year or less produce short-term capital gains; gains that occur in periods longer than one year are long-term capital gains. Short-term and long-term capital gains are treated differently for tax purposes.

Capital gains (mutual fund): The gain that is triggered when a mutual fund is sold for more than its initial purchase price. This gain is subject to the capital gain tax. Mutual funds do not pay tax on the gains in their portfolios; the law requires that 98 percent of the fund's capital gains be distributed to shareholders in the fund, who in turn pay the tax on the gain.

Capital loss: A loss resulting from the sale of tangible property. Losses are categorized as long- or short-term.

Cash: Coins and currency that is readily available.

Cash dividend: A dividend paid in cash to a company's shareholders. The amount is normally based on profitability and is taxable as income.

Cash and equivalents: The value of assets that can be converted into cash immediately, as reported by a company. Usually includes bank accounts and marketable securities, such as government bonds and banker's acceptances.

Certificate of Deposit (CD): Interest-bearing debt instrument that is issued by a bank.

Certified Financial Planner: Financial planner who has completed coursework and passed an exam in areas such as finance, insurance, and taxes.

Chartered Financial Consultant (ChFC): Financial planner who has taken classes in insurance, taxation real estate, economics, and insurance.

Closed-end funds: A mutual fund that does not accept new money and that does not issue new shares following the fund's initial public offering. Investors must purchase or sell their closed-end shares on the securities exchanges.

Collateral: Assets pledged by a borrower to a lender in order to secure a loan. If the debtor defaults, the lender can seize the collateral in lieu of payment.

Collateralized Mortgage Obligation (CMO): A bond that uses mortgages as collateral. It separates *mortgage pools* into different *maturity* classes called tranches.

Commercial paper: A short-term debt instrument issued by corporations. Its rate of interest is set at issuance and can be realized only if held to maturity.

Commission: The fee paid to a brokerage firm to execute a trade.

Common stock: A security issued that represents ownership of a corporation. Common stockholders may vote for the management and receive dividends after all other obligations of the corporation are satisfied.

Compound interest: Interest earned on, or assessed against, both an original investment and the interest already accrued. When interest is compounded, the value of an investment can increase dramatically over long periods of time.

Consumer Price Index (CPI): A measure of the prices of consumer goods and services and of the pace of U.S. inflation. The U.S. Department of Labor publishes the CPI every month.

Corporate bonds: Debt obligations issued by corporations.

Coupon: On bearer bonds, the detachable part of the certificate exchangeable for interest.

Coupon rate: In bonds, notes, or other fixed-income securities, the stated percentage rate of interest, usually paid twice a year.

Coverdell Education Savings Account: Formerly known as an Education IRA, an account that's set up on behalf of a child under 18 years of age to save for his or her college education.

Creation unit: A large block of 25,000 to 300,000 shares that forms the basic structure of an open-ended, exchange-traded fund. The huge block of shares is broken up and sold to institutional investors, who sell on the secondary market to retail investors.

Credit risk (also called default risk): The chance that a bond issuer will default on its obligation to pay interest and repay principal.

Default: An issuer's failure to pay accreted interest when a zero-coupon issue matures. Treasury securities are considered default-free.

Default risk (see Credit risk)

Deficit financing: The issuance and sale of bonds for the purpose of paring down other debt.

Defined benefit plan: A company pension plan that guarantees participants a specific retirement income benefit based on some particular formula. The formula is usually based on years of service.

Defined contribution plan: A company retirement plan that provides employees the opportunity to set aside before-tax income to save for retirement.

Diamonds: An exchange-traded fund structured as a trust that holds the 30 stocks in the Dow Jones Industrial Average. Each share represents a fraction of each of these large companies. Diamonds trade on the American Stock Exchange.

Discount: When the market price of a newly issued security is lower than the issue price.

Distributions: Payments of fund earnings (dividends) or gains (capital gains). Distributions can be made by check or by investing in additional shares. Funds are required to distribute gains (if any) to shareholders at least once per year.

Diversification: The process of dividing investments among a variety of securities having different risks and rewards so as to minimize risk.

Dividend reinvestment: Reinvestment of shareholder dividends into more shares of a company's stock.

Dividend Reinvestment Plan (also DRIP or DRP): Automatic reinvestment of shareholder dividends in more shares of a company's stock. Dividend reinvestment plans allow shareholders to accumulate capital over the long-term using dollar-cost averaging.

Dividends: A portion of a corporation's earnings paid to stockholders on a per-share basis. Most preferred stock pays a regular and prescribed dividend amount. If sufficient earnings remain after the preferred stockholders are paid, a dividend may be declared for common stockholders. Common stock dividend payments vary in amounts when declared.

Dogs of the Dow: Investment strategy in which you buy the 10 highest-yielding stocks on the Dow Jones Industrial Average.

Dollar-cost averaging: The practice of investing a fixed dollar amount at regular intervals.

Dow Jones Industrial Average (DJIA): The best-known and most widely accepted U.S. index of stocks, containing 30 stocks that trade on the New York Stock Exchange. Also known as the Dow, it is a barometer of how shares of the largest U.S. companies are performing.

Downtick: A listed equity trade whose price is lower than that of the last different sale.

Earnings per share (EPS): The net income divided by the number of shares of common stock outstanding.

Emerging markets: Securities in underdeveloped countries; stocks of companies in these areas have tremendous potential yet are volatile and have a high degree of risk.

Equity: 1. The value of the common stockholders' ownership in a company as listed on the balance sheet.
2. An investment that involves ownership, as opposed to a loan such as a bond or IOU; often used interchangeably with "stock."
3. With regards to a margin account, the investor's portion of ownership.

Equity-income funds: Mutual funds that focus on income and invest in large-company stocks that pay big dividends. If equity-income funds generate capital gains, it is usually that stocks, purchased at depressed prices, have become fully valued.

Eurodollar: U.S. currency held by a foreign bank, usually in Europe.

Event risk: The possibility that a bond rating will drop due to an event, such as a takeover, the taking on of additional debt, or a company recapitalization.

Exchange: The marketplace in which shares, options, and futures on stocks, bonds, commodities, and indexes are traded. Principal U.S. stock exchanges are: New York Stock Exchange (NYSE), American Stock

Exchange (AMEX), and the National Association of Securities Dealers (NASD).

Exchange-traded fund (ETF): An investment company structured as a mutual fund or trust that tracks an index, industry, or sector and is traded like a stock.

Expense ratio: The percentage of the assets that were spent to run a mutual fund (as of the last annual statement). This includes expenses such as management fees and overhead costs.

Face value: The debt (or loan) amount that appears on the face of the certificate and that the issuer must pay at maturity.

Fannie Mae: Nickname for the Federal National Mortgage Association and the mortgage-backed securities it issues.

Federal Reserve Board: The governing body of the Federal Reserve System. Board member actions help shape government monetary policy, most notably interest rates, for the U.S. economy.

Federal Housing Administration (FHA): The FHA is a government-sponsored agency that insures mortgage loans.

Federal Deposit Insurance Corporation (FDIC): A federal agency that guarantees the funds in bank and thrift deposit accounts up to $100,000.

Fitch Ratings (formerly Fitch's Investor Service): Firm that rates insurance companies as well as the creditworthiness of bonds and other securities issued by corporations and municipalities.

Fixed annuity: Guaranteed payments of a known and fixed dollar amount to the annuitant for the period covered under the contract.

Freddie Mac: Nickname for the Federal Home Mortgage Association and the mortgage-backed securities it issues.

Fund family: A group of individual mutual funds managed by a single company.

Fund manager: The person who determines how mutual fund assets are invested.

Futures: Agreement to buy or sell a predetermined amount of a commodity or financial instrument at a certain price on a stipulated date.

Ginnie Mae: Nickname for the Government National Mortgage Association and the mortgage-backed securities it issues.

Government bond: Debt security issued by the U.S. government.

Government National Mortgage Association (GNMA): A government corporation that provides primary mortgages through bond issuances. Its securities are called Ginnie Maes.

Government Sponsored Entity (GSE): An association chartered or sponsored by the federal government.

Growth and income funds: Mutual funds that invest in companies whose earnings are expected to grow, but which still pay good dividends. These funds may sacrifice some future profits in order to provide current income.

Growth at a Reasonable Price (GARP): Investment strategy that favors growth stocks that are reasonably priced compared to the overall market.

Growth stock: The stock of a company whose business possesses an above-average growth rate.

Hedge: To reduce the risk in one security by taking an offsetting position in a related security.

High-yield bond: A bond with a speculative credit rating of BB (S&P) or Ba (Moody's) or lower is a high-yield bond. These bonds offer higher yields for investors compared to bonds of financially sound companies.

Holding Company Depository Receipts (HOLDR): This is a type of security similar to an exchange-traded fund that represents a basket of securities from a single sector or industry. HOLDRs were created by Merrill Lynch and are traded on the American Stock Exchange.

Income: The portion of investment return that derives from interest or dividend payments.

Income funds: 1. Funds that focus on a variety of income-oriented securities.
   2. Mutual funds that invest in stocks and bonds earning regular dividends or interest.

Income stock: Common stock that typically pays a high dividend on a regular basis.

Index fund: A mutual fund whose portfolio matches that of a broad-based index such as Standard and Poor's 500 Index, and whose performance therefore mirrors the market or a particular market segment.

Individual Retirement Account (IRA): A tax-deferred savings plan. Contributions may be tax-deductible. All distributions are subject to tax when withdrawn.

Inflation: The rate at which the general level of prices for goods and services is rising.

Inflation risk: The risk that rising inflation will diminish the rate of real return an investor will realize over time.

Initial Public Offering (IPO): A company's first sale of stock to the public.

Insider: A person with nonpublic information on a corporation. Directors, officers, and stockholders owning more than 10 percent of any one class of stock are usually considered insiders.

Interest: The cost of borrowing money expressed as a percentage rate over a specified amount of time. Also, a share or title in property.

Interest rate: The amount charged by a lender for borrowing money, not including fees. Interest rates are generally fixed at a certain level for the entire length of a loan, though they can also vary over time.

Interest rate risk: The prospect that Treasury and agency securities will decline in price if economy-wide interest rates rise.

Intermediate-term bonds: Bonds with maturities of four to 10 years.

International funds: Mutual funds that invest money *outside* the United States. Some international funds invest in one area of the world. *Global* funds invest in companies in many different countries, including the United States.

Investment Advisor (also Registered Investment Advisor): The individual or firm that is responsible for managing a portfolio or mutual fund. Registered investment advisors undergo extensive training and have a minimum amount of experience in financial planning. They also have sworn to adhere to a code of ethics.

Investment horizon (time horizon): The length of time an individual plans to hold an investment. The longer the investment horizon, the more risk an investor can afford to take, and the higher returns you can earn.

Issue: 1. The process by which a new security is brought to market. 2. Any security.

IRA: See Individual Retirement Account

Junk bonds (also high-risk bonds): Bonds issued when the ability of the issuing company to pay interest is questioned. They are speculative instruments that pay high rates of interest.

Keogh plan: Tax-deferred retirement plan for a self-employed person.

Laddering: Investment strategy that seeks to hedge interest rate changes by buying bonds or CDs with maturities that are one or two years apart.

Large-cap stocks: Stocks issued by companies that are valued at over $5 billion.

Limit order: An order that sets the highest price the client is willing to pay for a buy order, or the lowest price the client is willing to accept for a sell order. Buy orders may be executed at or below the limit price, but never higher. Sell orders may be executed at or above the limit price, but never lower.

Liquidity: 1. The degree of ease with which an investor can convert an asset into cash.

2. The characteristic of a market that enables investors to buy and sell securities easily.

Load: A special sales charge (above normal transaction fees) assessed upon initial investment in or redemption of a mutual fund.

Load fund: A mutual fund with shares sold at a price including a sales charge. These funds are usually purchased through a financial advisor or some other salesperson.

Long-term bond: Bonds that mature in more than 10 years.

Management fees: The component of a fund's expense ratio that refers to the percentage of a fund's net assets paid to the fund's advisor; the firm primarily responsible for a fund's day-to-day operation.

Margin: 1. Purchasing Treasury and agency securities with money borrowed from a bank or brokerage.

2. The amount of equity contributed by the investor to purchase and hold marginable securities in a margin account.

Margin call: A demand upon a client to deposit money or securities with the broker when the value of the securities purchased on margin falls.

Market capitalization: Also known as market cap. The total dollar value of all outstanding shares. Computed as the number of shares multiplied by the current market price.

Market maker: Another term for dealer or specialist who stands ready to trade against the public and therefore make a market in an issue.

Market order: An order to be executed at the best available market price when received by the exchange or market maker. The order instructs the immediate execution of the trade without regard to price.

Matching: In some 401(k) plans, an employer provides a contribution that fully or partially matches the contribution of employees.

Maturity date: The date on which a loan, bond, or other debt instrument becomes due and payable.

Mid-cap stocks: Stocks of medium-sized companies. They offer growth potential with the stability of a larger company.

Money market deposit account: A bank or thrift savings account, that is similar to a money market fund, except that the depositor's assets are insured by the FDIC, up to $100,000.

Money market fund: A type of mutual fund that invests in high-quality, short-term debt instruments, such as T-bills and commercial paper, with maturities of 13 months or less. According to SEC rules, the average maturity for a money market fund may not exceed 90 days.

Money market instruments: Short-term debt instruments (such as U.S. Treasury bills, commercial paper, and banker's acceptances) that reflect current interest rates and that, because of their short life, do not respond to interest rate changes as longer-term instruments do.

Moody's Investor Service: Firm that rates the creditworthiness of bonds and other securities

Mortgage-backed securities: A collection of mortgages bundled into a single security and retailed to private or institutional investors as a single security.

Muni: Short for municipal bond.

Municipal bond: A long-term debt instrument issued by a state or local government. It usually carries a fixed rate of interest, which is paid semi-annually.

Municipal bond funds: Funds that invest in bonds issued by state and local governments.

Mutual fund (open-end): An investment firm that continuously offers new shares to investors of its portfolio. The mutual fund portfolio is invested in accordance to the objectives stated in the mutual fund's prospectus.

National Association of Securities Dealers (NASD): A self-regulating authority whose members, including OTC broker/dealers, establish standard business practices in addition to legal and ethical conduct.

National Association of Securities Dealers Automated Quotation System (NASDAQ): A communication network used to store and access quotations for qualified over-the-counter securities.

Net asset value (NAV): The dollar value of a mutual fund's underlying assets minus the fund's liabilities divided by the fund's number of shares outstanding.

New York Stock Exchange (NYSE): Located at 11 Wall Street, New York, New York, a market for buying and selling securities.

No-load: A mutual fund that does not require the payment of special sales commissions above regular transaction fees.

North American Securities Administrators Association (NASAA): The oldest international organization dedicated to investor protection (www.nasaa.org).

Note: The general name for a Treasury or agency security with an initial maturity of fewer than 10 years.

Option: A contract that entitles the buyer to buy (call) or sell (put) a predetermined quantity of an underlying security for a specific period of time at a preestablished price.

Par: Face value; the nominal value of a security.

Pension fund: A fund established for the payment of retirement benefits.

Phantom interest: The yearly-accreted interest that a zero-coupon security is presumed to pay each year it is held, even though payment of interest isn't made until the security matures.

Portfolio: 1. An individual's or institution's combined investment holdings, including cash, stocks, bonds, mutual funds, and real estate.

2. A group of investments held by a single person or entity. Portfolios may include any number or type of investment, from real estate holdings to high-tech stocks.

Portfolio turnover: The percentage of a fund's portfolio that is sold in any given year.

Preferred stock: Stock that represents ownership in the issuing corporation and that has prior claim on dividends. In the case of bankruptcy, preferred stock has a claim on assets ahead of common stockholders. The expected dividend is part of the issue's description.

Premium bond: A note or bond selling at a price above par.

Price/Book ratio: Compares a stock's market value to the value of total assets less total liabilities (book). Determined by dividing current price by common stockholders' equity per share (book value), adjusted for stock splits.

Price/Earnings ratio (PE): 1. The current share price divided by the last published earnings per share, where earnings per share is net profit divided by the number of ordinary shares.

2. Shows the "multiple" of earnings at which a stock sells. Determined by dividing current price by current earnings per share (adjusted for stock splits). Earnings per share for the P/E ratio is determined by dividing earnings for the past 12 months by the number of common shares outstanding.

Private activity: Nonessential municipal business dealings—as opposed to municipal business—that can trigger the Alternative Minimum Tax in a municipal bond or municipal bond fund.

QQQQ (Cubes): The exchange-traded fund based on the NASDAQ 100 Index.

Rate of return: The percentage gain or loss for a mutual fund in a specific time period. This number assumes that all distributions are reinvested at the current rate of return. Annualized return is a compounded yearly rate.

Rating: The alphabetical designation attesting to the investment quality of a bond. Treasury and agency securities that are AAA-rated are said to be "investment grade."

Rebalancing: Making adjustments to a portfolio so that assets are in the same proportions as in your original asset allocation.

Redemption charge: The commission charged by a mutual fund when redeeming shares. For example, a 2 percent redemption charge (also called a "back-end load") on the sale of shares valued at $1,000 will result in payment of $980 (or 98 percent of the value) to the investor. This charge may decrease as shares are held for longer time periods.

Real Estate Investment Trust (REIT): A company that purchases or manages real estate and long-term mortgages.

Return: The money that an investment earns over a certain period of time. Lower-risk investments generally earn low or moderate returns. Higher returns require investors to take more risk.

Risk: The inherent possibility that an investment will lose value. In general, the more risk an investor is willing to take, the more money he or she can make from an investment, especially over the long term.

Roth IRA: A savings plan like the traditional IRA, except contributions are not tax-deductible and qualified distributions are tax-free from federal tax.

Russell 2000 Index: Measures the performance of 2,000 small-cap stocks.

Sallie Mae: Nickname for the Student Loan Marketing Association and the securities it issues.

Secondary market: The market in which securities are traded after the initial (or primary) offering, gauged by the number of issues traded. The over-the-counter market is the largest secondary market.

Sector funds: Mutual funds that invest in specific industries, such as entertainment, energy, or finance. Sector funds are generally higher-risk investments because of their lack of diversity.

Securities: A general term used to describe any kind of investment product, though it can also refer specifically to stocks and bonds.

Securities and Exchange Commission (SEC): The federal agency responsible for the enforcement of laws governing the securities industry.

Selling short: An investment strategy where the investor sells a stock he or she does not own with the intention of buying it back later at a lower price.

Simplified Employee Pension Plan (SEP): A pension plan in which both employees and employers contribute to a tax-deferred IRA. SEPs are geared toward self-employed people or owners of companies with fewer than 25 employees.

Series EE savings bond: A Treasury bond sold at half of par, this type of savings bond matures in 12 years.

Shareholder: A person or entity that owns a share or shares in a corporation.

Sharpe ratio: A measure of how much risk must be taken in order to reap a certain return.

Short-term bond: A bond that matures within five years.

Short-term bond funds: Funds that invest in bonds with average maturities of three years or less.

Short-term government bond: A government bond that matures in one to five years.

Sinking fund: A fund into which a company sets aside money in order to retire its preferred stock, bonds, or debentures.

Small-cap stocks: Stocks issued by companies that are valued at less than $1 billion. Small-cap stocks can offer high-growth opportunities, but often pay small dividends or none at all.

Small-company funds: Funds that invest in companies that generally have an average of $500 million or less in market capitalization.

Spread: The difference between the bid and offer sides of a quote.

Standard & Poor's Depository Receipt ("SPDR" or "SPIDER"): An exchange-traded fund structured as a unit investment trust that holds a portfolio of stock that tracks the performance of the S&P 500.

Standard & Poor's 500: A broad-based measure of the stock market conditions weighted on market value and based on the performance of 500 widely-held stocks.

Stop order: A protective order that becomes a market order when the price is reached or passed. Buy stops are entered above the current market price; sell stops are entered below it.

Standard deviation: A statistical measure used to calculate a fund or portfolio's volatility and how much it deviates from the average.

Stock: A share in the ownership of a company. A company's stocks can be issued privately or may be traded publicly through a stock exchange.

Stop order: A proective order that becomes a market order when the price is reached or passed. Buy stops are entered about the current market price; sell stops are entered below it.

STRIPS (Separate Trading of Registered Interest and Principal of Securities): *U.S. Treasury* bond that has separated its two components, *interest* and *principal*, and then sold them individually.

Taxable equivalent yield: The *yield* before factoring in taxes. It's equal to after-tax yield divided by (1 minus the tax rate).

Tax-exempt bonds: Municipal securities whose interest is free from federal income tax.

T-bills (Treasury bills): Obligations issued by the Department of the Treasury maturing in 13, 26, or 52 weeks.

Term (loan): The amount of time in which a loan must be repaid in full.

Ticker symbol: A designated letter abbreviation for a publicly traded company. These symbols are usually between one and four letters. Mutual fund abbreviations are five letters.

Time horizon (Investment Horizon): The expected length of time an investor allows in order to meet financial goals.

TIPS (Treasury Inflation-Protected Securities): U.S. Treasury bonds that are pegged to changes in the consumer price index so the yield rises to offset the effects of inflation.

Trade: A verbal or electronic transaction involving one party buying a security from another party.

Treasury bills (see T-bills).

Treasury bond: A long-term (10 to 30 years), fixed-interest government debt security.

Treasury direct: The program through which investors may purchase new issues of Treasury bills, notes, and bonds directly from the Federal Reserve.

Treasury note: A medium-term (1 to 10 years), fixed-interest government debt security.

Turnover ratio: A measure of a mutual fund manager's trading activity during the previous year. This is expressed as a percentage of the average total assets of the fund. A turnover ratio of 25 percent means that the value of trades represented one-fourth of the assets of the fund.

Underwriter (Investment Banker): In a municipal underwriting, a brokerage firm or bank that acts as a conduit by taking the new issue from the municipality and reselling it. In a corporate offering, the underwriter must be a brokerage firm.

Uniform Gift to Minors Account (UGMA): A method of securities ownership whereby parents or other relatives may contribute cash or securities to children. Portions of returns generated by the securities are taxed at the children's tax bracket instead of the parents' presumably higher bracket.

Unit Investment Trust (UIT): Pools of money collected from individuals and invested in stocks, bonds, or other property to produce an income stream. Investors receive shares representing their contribution to the pool. The assets held in a UIT are not traded; they remain fixed until they mature or the trust is liquidated.

Uptick: A listed equity trade at a price that is higher than that of the last sale.

Uptick rule: An SEC rule that states that in most circumstances no short sale may be made when the last trade on the security was a down-tick.

Value fund: A *mutual fund* that invests in companies that are considered to be underpriced relative to their anticipated future value. The fund looks to buy companies that have fallen out of favor for any number of reasons, sometimes it's due to public relations problems, poor earnings believed to be temporary, or other short-lived circumstances.

Value stock: A stock that is considered to be a high-quality company at a cheap price.

VIPER: The acronym for Vanguard Index Participation Equity Receipts. This is a variation of an exchange-traded fund in that instead of tracking an index, it tracks the Vanguard Total Stock Market Index Fund. It's considered a share class of that fund.

Volatility: A relative measure of a security's price movement during a given time period. It is measured mathematically by the annual standard deviation of daily stock price changes.

Wash-Sale Rule: The Wash-Sale Rule prevents taxpayers (nondealers) from selling securities at a loss and reacquiring "substantially identical" securities within a 30-day period before or after a loss. The Internal Revenue Service has taken the position that the Wash-Sale Rule will disallow a loss on the sale of the security.

Wilshire 5000 Equity Index: A market value-weighted index that includes all NYSE and AMEX stocks and the most active over-the-counter stocks.

Yield: The percentage rate of return paid on a stock in the form of dividends, or the effective rate of interest paid on a bond or note.

Yield curve: A curve plotted on a graph showing the relation of interest rates to yields to maturity on Treasury obligations. A *normal* yield curve shows an upward slope indicating that long-term bonds have higher yields than short-term bonds. In rare circumstances, the curve is the *inverse* of the usual slope, showing that long-term interest rates are lower than short-term; this is an anomaly and usually signals declining rates. If there is little difference between short- and long-term yields, the yield curve is *flat*.

Zero-coupon bonds: A bond sold at a fraction of its par or face value. There are no periodic interest payments, but it appreciates and the holder receives face value upon its maturity.

Z-tranches: The last class of bonds in a collateralized mortgage obligation (CMO). They accrue interest periodically but there are no cash payments until earlier tranches in the same CMO have been retired.

NOTES

Chapter 1

1. Securities Industry Association, "Equity Ownership in America" (2002).
2. *DowJones.com.*
3. Morningstar, Inc., as of 9/28/04.
4. Morningstar, Inc., as of 9/27/04.
5. Jonathan Pond, C.P.A., president of Financial Planning Information, Inc., and author of *Your Money Matters, 21 Tips for Achieving Financial Security in the 21st Century.*

Chapter 2

1. *The Money-Making Guide to Bonds*, by Hildy Richelson and Stan Richelson (Bloomberg Press, 2002).
2. Federal Reserve (annual disclosure forms, published in 2003 for the year 2002).
3. TreasuryDirect, Bureau of the Public Debt, U.S. Department of the Treasury, *www.publicdebt.treas.gov*, as of 9/28/04.

Chapter 3

1. *Bankrate.com*, as of 7/28/04.
2. *www.creditunion.coop/ratedex.php*, as of 9/27/04.

3. *Bankrate.com* as of 7/28/04.

4. *Bankrate.com*, as of 7/28/04.

5. National Association of Credit Unions; *www.cuna.coop.*

6. iMoneyNet.

7. iMoneyNet.

8. iMonetNet.

9. "Bank and Thrift Regulation," by William S. Haraf, *Regulation, The Cato Review of Business & Government*, The Cato Institute.

10. National Association of Credit Unions and iMoneyNet.

11. *Bankrate.com*, as of 9/27/04.

12. *Bankrate.com*, as of 7/27/04.

13. "Corporate MMAs Offer Good Rates But No Safety Net" by Laura Bruce, *Bankrate.com*, August 23, 2004.

Chapter 4

1. Massachusetts Financial Services' Historical Archives, "50 Years of Trust" (1974).

2. Mutual Fund Education Alliance.

3. Mutual Fund Education Alliance's Investor Center at MFEA.com.

4. Mutual Fund Education Alliance.

5. Morningstar, Inc., as of 8/3/04.

6. Growth rates.

7. Lipper, Inc., as of 9/28/04.

8. Morningstar, Inc. 8/3/04.

9. Morningstar., Inc. 8/3/04.

10. Morningstar, Inc. 8/3/04.

11 Ted Aronson of institutional money management firm, Aronson + Johnson + Ortiz, in Philadelphia, Pennsylvania.

12. *Barron's*, April 2, 1990, p. 15.

13. Morningstar.

Chapter 5

1. "Fateful Meeting Launched U.S. ETFs—Inventor Credits Index-fund Pioneer for Push," by John Spence, *CBS.MarketWatch.com*, June 6, 2004.
2. *All About Exchange-Traded Funds* by Archie Richards, Jr. (McGraw-Hill, 2003).
3. *IndexUniverse.com* and *ETFconnect.com*.
4. Morningstar, Inc.
5. Morningstar, Inc.
6. Morningstar, Inc.
7. "ETFs: Mutual Funds for the 21st Century," by Suze Orman, Yahoo Personal Finance's *Money Matters*.
8. *The Lazy Person's Guide to Investing* by Paul B. Farrell, J.D., Ph.D. (Warner Books, 2004).

Chapter 6

1. Retirement Confidence Survey, Employee Benefits Research Institute, April 5, 2002.
2. Social Security Administration's Period Life Table 2001 (updated 6/16/04).
3. David Wray, President of the Profit-sharing/401(k) Council of America.
4. David Wray, President of the Profit-sharing/401(k) Council of America.
5. United States Department of Education.
6. Joseph Hurley, Founder and CEO of *SavingforCollege.com*.
7. Progressive Casualty Insurance Company, January 22, 2002.
8. Experian Consumer Direct, August 18, 2004.

Chapter 7

1. Duncan Richardson, manager of Eaton Vance Tax-managed Growth Fund.
2. Morningstar, as of August 24, 2004 [contact: Annette Larson, Senior Research Analyst].

3. *Morningstar.com.*

4. *Mary Farrell's Beyond the Basics* by Mary Farrell (Simon & Schuster, 2000).

Chapter 8

1. "Determinants of Portfolio Performance" and "Determinants of Portfolio Performance II: An Update" by Gary P. Brinson, Brian D. Singer and Gilbert L. Beebower, both published in the *Financial Analysts Journal*, July/August 1986 and May/June 1991, respectively.

2. Social Security Administration's Period Life Table 2001 (updated updated 6/16/04).

Chapter 9

1. *The Truth About Money* by Ric Edelman, (HarperCollinsPublishers, 1996, 1998).

Chapter 10

1. *Rich Dad's Guide to Investing* by Robert T. Kiyosaki with Sharon L. Lechter (Warner Books, 2000).

2. Securities & Exchange Commission.

3. National Association of Personal Financial Advisors.

4. Dalbar, Inc.'s study of investor behavior, April 1, 2004. Examining the flows into and out of mutual funds for the last 20 years, the Dalbar study found that market timers in stock mutual fund lost 3.29 percent per year on average. Over a period when the S&P grew by 12.98 percent, the average investor earned only 3.51 percent.

5. *Data Driven Investing—Professional Edition* by Bill Matson and Mitch Hardy (Data Driven Publishing, 2004) *Datadrivenpublishing.com.*

6. Fifth annual Phoenix Wealth Survey conducted by The Phoenix Companies, Inc., Hartford, Connecticut.

7. From *Does Your Broker Owe You Money?* by Dan Solin (Alpha Press, 2003).

RESOURCES

Chapter 1

www.Bloomberg.com
www.CBSMarketwatch.com
www.Dripinvestor.com
www.Financialengines.com
www.fool.com
www.Investools.com
www.investor.reuters.com
www.Moneycentral.com
www.Morningstar.com
www.JonathanPond.com
www.SmartMoney.com
www.Standardandpoors.com
www.TheStreet.com
www.ValueLine.com
www.Zacks.com

Chapter 3

www.bankrate.com
www.caterpillar.com or 800-504-1114
www.demandnotes.com or 888-271-4066
www.geinterestplus.com or 800-433-4480

www.ici.org
www.iMoneyNet.org
www.money-rates.com

Chapter 4

www.ici.org
www.indexfunds.com
www.indexrx.com
www.indexuniverse.com
www.investorama.com
www.lipper.com
www.mfea.com
www.morningstar.com
www.mutuals.com
www.naic.com
www.profunds.com
www.rydexfunds.com
www.standardandpoors.com
www.valueline.com

Chapter 5

www.efficientfrontier.com
www.etfconnect.com
www.ETFMarket.com
www.frescoshares.com
www.holdrs.com
www.indexuniverse.com
www.ishares.com
www.journalofindexes.com
www.nuveen.com
www.spdrindex.com
www.ssga.com
www.vanguard.com

Chapter 6

www.campusconsultants.com
www.CardWeb.com
www.choosetosave.org
www.collegeboard.org
www.collegesavings.org
www.debtsmart.com
www.eloan.com
www.fafsa.ed.gov
www.financialaid.com
www.fool.com
www.LendingTree.com
www.mapping-your-future.org
www.myFICO.com
www.petersons.com
www.salliemae.com
www.savingforcollege.org
www.upromise.com
www.wiredscholar.com

Chapter 7

www.kiplinger.com
www.moneycentral.com
www.riskgrades.com
www.vanguard.com

Chapter 8

www.ebri.org
www.ici.org
www.investopedia.com
www.moneycentral.com
www.morningstar.com
www.vanguard.com

Chapter 9

www.assetallocation.org
www.enterprise529.com
www.kiplinger.com
www.morningstar.com
www.ricedelman.com
www.vanguard.com

Chapter 10

www.amercoll.edu
www.cfp.net
www.fpanet.org
www.napfa.org
www.nasaa.org
www.nasd.org
www.sec.gov

INDEX